I0827107

The Uncomfortable History of Christianity

By Andrew Linnell

Threefold Publishing

Seattle, WA.

ISBN: 978-1-7363165-9-7

Front cover image by Andrew Linnell.
Book design by Andrew Linnell.

Published by Threefold Publishing
United States of America.

First published edition 2020.

Threefold Publishing
P.O. Box 251
Mountlake Terrace, WA 98043

www.cfae.us/threefold-publishing

Contents

Acknowledgements

Many come to mind to whom I would like to express my sincere gratitude. But, as I write this after many years of research and just before publication, I am sure I will have forgotten some whose contributions were important to this book. I am very sorry to have not mentioned these.

Supporting my efforts to compose this book has been my dear wife Natasha who has been my first reader for each section, my most listened to critic, and my principal cheerleader. Her unflinching support for me and this project persisted over these past four years of writing. While I closed my office door to keep out the cats, she prepared sustenance and insights that kept this effort rolling along.

My uncle and head of the Rochester-Colgate Divinity School, John Charles Wynn, brought to me an interest in the history of the Christian religion. Our families gathered for Thanksgivings throughout my childhood. His warmth and joy when asked questions about Christianity filled my soul with inspiration to pursue this work.

The minister who oversaw my confirmation class as a child whose name I no longer recall, took the members of his class to services at other churches so that we could confidently say "I want to be a member of this church" when asked on Confirmation Sunday. My family church was the First Congregational Church in Amherst, MA.

Neill Reilly brought his catholic education and persuasion as he adeptly reviewed the original manuscript. He found numerous areas where my composition needed more explanation or more careful theological claims. My appreciation for his review is deep and personally gratifying. Our frequent discussions on Christianity have been remarkably helpful.

Preface.

As the son of a professor of Astronomy, I grew up with an inherited deference for the academic. My dad, the son of a minister, took the family to church every Sunday. He sang in the choir. Over my boyhood years, the question was often asked "why do we go to church? Is it not in conflict with Science?" For a while, faith and knowledge kept their distance and this question was whisked away. Eventually, however, as my dad eased into his 70s, the importance of going to church was lost to him. For me, I never joined a church as a member. Over my life, I have attended a number of churches, but I found them to be more social clubs than a church. I used to remark that I've never found a church that would have me as a member with my beliefs intact." My children, therefore, missed out on this religious experience. I tried to supplement for it at home, but I sense I failed. I do hope that they gained a sense for the hallowedness of certain spaces and could find reverence for what is worthy of being revered.

As an engineering student at the University of Michigan, Ann Arbor, I considered myself "different". To prove this, at least to myself, I would often sit in to listen to lectures in art history or philosophy. I got up my courage to take a philosophy course, but I took it Pass/Fail. I got an A+ and was clearly loved by my professor. Philosophy stuck with me after this class.

With this background, I carried questions about philosophy and Christian theology throughout my life. One author who can set the philosophical and theological mood of Early Christians would be the Jewish philosopher, Philo of Alexandria who wrote, "And do not thou ever cease through weariness to anoint thy eyes until you have introduced those who are duly initiated to the secret light of the sacred scriptures and have displayed to them the hidden things therein contained, and their reality, which is invisible to those who are uninitiated. It is becoming then for you to act thusly; but as for ye, O souls, who have once tasted of divine love, as if you had even awakened from deep sleep, dissipate the mist that is before you." What was this about? What was it to be "duly initiated"? What was this "secret light" and were the "sacred scriptures" something more than the Bible?

Philo continued, "Now of these souls some descend upon the earth with a view to be bound up in mortal bodies, those namely which are most nearly connected with the earth, and which are lovers of the body. But some soar upwards, being again distinguished according to the definitions and times which have been appointed by nature. Of these, those which are influenced by a desire for mortal life, and which have been familiarized to it, again return to it."[1] What was the image of the Human Being back in Philo's time? What is there beyond the physical body?

Philo speaks here of concepts such as reincarnation as well as initiation in the mysteries. Such topics were avoided or barely glanced upon during those undergraduate classes that I attended at the University of Michigan. I listened and learned all I could from such classes, but I felt something was missing. It would be years later, in 1975, when I was forced by my girlfriend to attend a conference on nutrition with her in Spring Valley, NY. Before going, I had convinced myself that this was for her and I needed to

---

[1] Philo, "On Dreams" (1.164; 1.138-1.139), http://www.earlyjewishwritings.com/text/philo/book21.html

find something to prove to her that this sponsoring group called Anthroposophy was unscientific and wacko regarding religious thought. I saw what I expected to be a goldmine for this endeavor: a bookstore. I went and found what I expected to be just the material I needed. The book was only $1, and it contained two lectures by Rudolf Steiner entitled The *True Nature of the Second Coming*. I was certain this would supply juicy material to prove that we should go home immediately. I started reading. 90 minutes later, I was a changed man. My entire orientation to religion and philosophy had been altered forever. Nothing had I ever read before or after had such a profound impact on my life. It was as if I was present at the lectures with how deeply they spoke to me.

The point of view of this book was intended as a narrator seeing Christian history as Leonardo da Vinci may have seen it. This is because this book was intended as a companion book to *The Hidden Heretic of the Renaissance: Leonardo* that showed how Leonardo da Vinci had revealed in his painting, the *Virgin of the Rocks*, what would have been considered a heresy in his time. The heresy revealed was that Christ was born at the baptism and that there were two boys, two messiahs, one kingly, one priestly, who prepared for this birth of Christ. One boy is discussed in the gospel attributed to Matthew while Luke describes the other boy. These two books enhance each other.

The Hidden Heretic of the Renaissance: Leonardo explained how the paintings *Virgin of*

the Rocks and several related paintings by Leonardo's students together reveal this heresy in the form of a mystery. That book led to the discovery that Leonardo's theme and the depictions are remarkably different from what art historians had hitherto speculated. To support the premise that Leonardo held theological views that would have been deemed heretical in his time, the book needed to survey Christian history and focus on those who were labeled heretics. That task has fallen to this, its companion book.

Bear in mind, Leonardo likely knew much of what you are about to read. This book will explore the evolution of the various theologies and philosophies present as Christianity began to take form. This book will follow the ebbs and flows of these up until the time Leonardo da Vinci was studying in Florence. It will look at how these streams of theology and philosophy shaped what emerged during the Renaissance.

Introduction

"In an altered age we worship the dead forms of our forefathers. The world holds onto a formal Christianity, and nobody dares to talk about the heart of Christianity, for fear of shocking."

Ralph Waldo Emerson [2]

This book traces this history, through the time when Christianity essentially became the religion of the Roman Empire to well after Rome fell and the Church had drifted deep into corruption. When we look at the Golden Age of Greece, before Rome and Christianity had entered the stage of history, we find that humanity believed that they were guided by inspirations attained through their ancient mystery centers. Such centers were found everywhere in the ancient world. Because ancient humanity learned through stories, not logical reasoning, the key inspirations from the mysteries became their instructive myths. Later, in Roman times, human laws replaced

---

[2] Ralph Waldo Emerson, Journals and Miscellaneous Notebooks 4:27

the teachings and stories (although such laws may have originated from these mystery centers). One can see by this transition from the experience of interactions with living gods to the rule of law, that human experience of a spiritual world had been fading away.

When Christianity began, the door to experiencing the spiritual world had largely shut. Even dreams no longer provided sound spiritual guidance. The mystery centers themselves, were no longer able to bring students to full initiation. These centers were fading away too. Although Early Christianity, in an attempt to formulate a new concept of moral freedom, proclaimed that Christ had fulfilled the Law. Later, the Church with imperial support would take on the role of defining moral laws. As humanity evolved, each individual came to stand, with the strength of their own intellect, independent of their bloodline. Now, since the Reformation, the individual is called upon to be their own guide, to use their own moral compass.

There is no intention of condemning a church or even individuals in this history. We can and should learn from this past. The purpose of this book is to paint the picture of what

Leonardo da Vinci and others faced during the Renaissance. As such, this is a companion book to *The Hidden Heretic of the Renaissance: Leonardo*.

Once, Art, Science, and Religion were one. But, by the time of Leonardo and the Renaissance, they were splitting apart. For Leonardo and his school, art still provided a path to reveal knowledge. Because of an active Inquisition, scientists had to be careful in what they revealed for fear of being labeled a heretic. They struggled with the question, "do I stand for Truth even if it might mean I forfeit my life?" Unlike his contemporary scientists, an artist such as Leonardo could more easily disguise unapproved concepts into a painting without an Inquisition sentencing him to the pyre.

Christianity within the Western Roman Empire (325 – 410)[3] and later within the Holy Roman Empire (800 – 1806) often acted more Imperial than Christian. It was a time when a monarch's

---

[3] The Eastern Roman Empire continued until Constantinople fell in 1253 to the Ottomans. This Eastern Roman Empire would reconquer Rome in 537 AD. Eastern Emperor Justinian replaced pro-Gothic Pope Silverius (536–537) with his own choice, Pope Vigilius (537–555).

benevolent rulership of a people had been infiltrated by egoism. Imperial rule by might overcame right. Rome would be taken back from the Ostrogoths in 537 by the Byzantine Emperor Justinian. Imperial domination of the papacy lasted from 537 to 752. This Byzantine Papacy required the approval of the Byzantine Emperor for the selection of a Roman pope. Justinian I appointed three successive popes. His successors continued this practice. Rome under the Greek popes constituted a "melting pot" of Western and Eastern Christian traditions, reflected in art as well as liturgy. During Byzantine Papacy, only Pope Martin I (649 – 655) questioned the authority of the Byzantine monarch to confirm the election of the Bishop of Rome. Imperial process became the process of governance within the Roman Church.

Much of what you are about to read may be uncomfortable for Christians or other religious individuals to read. This past is full of immoral deeds, of deceit, of yielding theology to politics, and of settling with theological differences through murder.

Because fifteenth century Florence was a cultural hub, its great artists and Leonardo da

Vinci in particular, certainly had ample opportunity to become aware of church and Christian history. This book is about an uncomfortable Christian history in which evolving philosophies and human failings play a major role for both the Orthodox and the Roman Catholic Churches. These human failings will be shown as steps or stages of humanity's collective moral development. Embedded in this book is a call for a Renaissance 2.0.

1. Europe at the Start of the Renaissance

We will begin by examining the state of Christianity and society in the thirteenth century. Interest in securing the Holy Lands through expensive crusades, popular in the eleventh century, was waning. The Middle Ages were coming to an end, to be swept away by the Bubonic Plague. A new culture and religious attitude were to arise.

The Christianity of Saint Francis

A figure of great importance to the era was Saint Francis of Assisi. To understand what St. Francis of Assisi brought to the Church is to understand how corrupt and immoral the Church had become. As a wealthy, spoiled youth, Francis's drinking and partying were legendary in his own time. But in 1202 war broke out between Assisi and Perugia. With his friends, Francis enrolled in the cavalry. Francis was captured in a battle and imprisoned for ransom. When the ransom was not paid, Francis remained for a year in prison. According to legend, prison changed him. While in his cell, he began receiving visions from God. Once released, Francis wandered in Italy. He came to the ruins of a church, San

Damiano. Here legend claims that he heard the voice of Christ tell him, “rebuild my Church.” After completing repairs to that building, he realized Christ had meant the Christian Church!

Because of the greed and avarice within the church (to which his own family was a part), Francis dedicated himself to a life of poverty.

Figure 1 St. Francis, Cimabue, ca. 1300

His reputation spread all over the Christian world. He traveled to Egypt with the Fifth Crusade of 1219 as the army's chaplain. While the Crusaders were encamped, he slipped across enemy lines to meet with the Egyptian leaders in the hopes of avoiding the battle. Apparently, he had even hoped to convert Malek al-Kamil, the Sultan himself to Christianity. "The two discussed interfaith conflict, war and the search for peace."[4] This drama was made into a documentary called "The Sultan and the Saint" that aired on December 26, 2017 on PBS.

Francis was canonized as a saint on July 16, 1228. Catholics and other Christians everywhere continue to revere him. But his rebuilding of the Church was only partially successful. Although his Franciscan order continued with their devotion to the poor, the Church hierarchy remained unchanged. By mid-fifteenth century, when Leonardo da Vinci was receiving his education, the old ways had fully reasserted themselves and could be said to have become even more corrupt.

---

[4] Mark Pattison, *The Jesuit Review America*, Catholic News Service, 8Dec2017

The Black Death

The catastrophe of the Black Plague dramatically changed European cultural life. During the fourteenth century, a bacterium carried by fleas on rodents removed from forty to sixty-five percent of the population of Western Europe and thirty to sixty percent of the population of all of Europe.[5] This pandemic took its biggest toll from 1347 to 1351 when well over a third of the population from the Italy to England died. People fled the cities. Constant fires burned the bodies of the continual flow of victims.

Because merchants carried goods infected with rodents, travelers of any kind became scorned. Thus, the Grand Era of Pilgrimages (tenth – fourteenth centuries) came to an end. Trekking the Way of St. James from the Pyrenees to Santiago de Compostela, or searching for the Holy Grail, or taking a sacred journey to the Holy Lands to walk to Golgotha, all such sacred pilgrimages essentially ceased. The Plague also finished off any hope of continuing the Era of Crusades (1096 to 1271).

---

[5] Suzanne Austin Alchon, *A pest in the land: new world epidemics in a global perspective*, University of New Mexico Press. p. 21, 2003.

Gone by the end of the fourteenth century, either as a result of the Plague or by imperial might, were the Cathars, the Knights Templar along with their institutions and infrastructures, as well as the great School at Chartres. The Albigensian Crusade of 1209–1229 destroyed with despicable cruelty the Cathars, a group whose Christian views did not submit to the Pope, nor did they see a subservient role for women, and their brotherly approach to society and economics stood out in stark contrast to the prevailing fiefdoms. More about the Cathars will come later in this book.

While the Plague raged, the population asked the clergy "why is God doing this to us? Can you not, through prayer, stop this Black Death?" Disillusionment with the Church grew not only in the people but in the priesthood as well. The Church in Rome's rule of the religious life appeared more and more as unmerciful might. The Inquisition that began to root out all sympathizers of the Cathars was called derogatorily "the hounds of God" by the peasantry. The Church reforms begun by St. Francis (1181 – 1226) became unrealizable legend.

Knights Templar

No group affected Europe's overall economy more than the Knights Templar. King Philip IV "the Fair" of France became deeply in debt to the Templars due to his endless wars. When a mob threatened to kill the unpopular king, perhaps because of his high taxes, he sought refuge in a Templar sanctuary. While there he envisioned that the Templars had huge hordes of gold for which he lusted. Prosperity had come to the Templars through their banking and their civil engineering.

In 1130, Gregorio Papareschi became Pope Innocent II through the strong support by the influential Bernard of Clairvaux. Following his rise to Pope Innocent II, he approved Bernard of Clairvaux's request to grant a new monk-warrior order to the Knights Templar. With Pope Innocent II's decree, the Templar Order needed to submit only to the Pope, not to any king. With this, they were also empowered to design and build churches across Europe. With selflessness they undertook this task with great vigor. No designer, no engineer, no worker signed their name to these impressive constructions.

Figure 2: West façade of Saint-Denis, Paris

The new architecture of the Gothic Cathedral[6] may be ascribed to these knights. They introduced this new style by 1134. Soon, all over Europe, Templars were planning and constructing churches according to their new architecture. Where did they learn such skills?

[6] See Alessandro Camiz, *Gothic, Frankish or Crusader? Reconsidering the origins of Gothic Architecture*, 2017

What was their inspiration? What mood did such a church provide to a congregant?

One of the first of these great cathedrals, Saint-Denis, was finished in 1144. After seeing this, Maurice de Sully, the Bishop of Paris, decided in 1160 to tear down the Romanesque cathedral Notre Dame in order to build a grand Gothic one. Work was underway by 1163.

To build such huge cathedrals, extra support was needed. The first Gothic cathedral to include flying buttresses within the original plan was Chartres. With this modification, the High Gothic period began with the new architecture and perfected building procedures.

Already admired for their selflessness and fearlessness in battle during the Crusades, constructing such cathedrals further endeared these Templar Knights to the populace. Thus, for King Philip IV to prevail over them and to seize their gold, he would need to strike secretly and quickly and then to sully their reputation. Philip urged his childhood friend, who he had ushered into the papacy as Pope Clement V, to at least put the Templars on trial for heresy.

It was common knowledge that King Philip IV of France had 'persuaded the cardinals' to select his childhood friend as the new Pope. Once installed, Philip then had Clement move the Papacy from Rome to Avignon, France where the king could ensure his control over the Church.

The order's downfall began on a Friday the 13th in 1307 when Philip executed a Gestapo-like round-up of the Templars. They were to be put on trial. But the pope could not find any support for the charge of heresy. They were then put under torture to get them to confess to their heresies.

While under torture, the Knights revealed unusual practices such as spitting on crosses and kissing during their initiation rites. During their trial in 1308, the Knights argued that the spitting was done to prepare themselves for what might happen if captured by the Saracens. Like the Kiss of Judas, this was done to show each candidate what in their soul was akin to Judas. The result was to be compassion for all. The process of initiation needed to reveal to each neophyte their own faults and weaknesses. They then knew what it was that they inwardly needed to overcome in order to accomplish complete obedience to the Ideals of the Order. The knights had confessed to the very things that they had overcome as part of their training and initiation. These became the basis for condemning them as heretics.

However, the Pope and his judges accepted this explanation and absolved them of heresy. That made Philip furious! His pressure finally prevailed on the Pope who consented to burn Jacques de Molay, the head of the order, and many of his closest associates at the stake. The king took what he could find of the order's riches while the surviving knights slipped away into Scotland and Portugal.

The famous last words of Jacques de Molay, spoken on March 18, 1314, were recorded! He said, “Pope Clement, Chevalier Guillaume de Nogaret, and King Philip! I summon you to the Tribunal of Heaven before the year is out!” Both the Pope and the King were indeed so summoned as both would be dead within the year! But it was believed by the peasantry, God’s wrath was not appeased. And so, as further punishment, He also sent the Plague.

Figure 3: King Philip presiding over the burning of the Templars, illustration in book by Giovanni Boccaccio, 1343

While the accusations and confessions may have led some people to wonder about Templar guilt, the torture and destruction of the knights was far too brutal for the common Christian. Moreover, the weakness of the Pope to defend his original judgement of innocence before the King thereby weakened the whole Roman Church.

The attempt at Templar extermination stimulated many legends about the order.[7] Some trace these knights to the Portuguese pirates and some to the Scottish Rites of Freemasonry. The claims that the Black Plague was God's retribution for the extermination of the Knights Templar raised them to legendary status. The populace had loved these Knights and what they stood for. The Church was deemed to be too weak to defend Christian values. Following King Philip IV and the Plague would come the questioning of the Church. People became fed up with its hierarchical obstinance, corruption, greed, and senseless politics. All this planted the Papacy itself deeply into crisis.

The Babylonian Captivity of the Papacy

Before his conflict with the Knights Templar, King Philip had been in conflict with a succession of Popes. One, Pope Boniface VIII was arrested by Philip. Boniface died from his torture in prison. The next Pope fared no better and apparently, in disfavor with Philip, died mysteriously perhaps by poisoning. When the next conclave met to select a Pope, the

---

[7] http://www.scrinium.org/en-us/Commission/Vatican-Secret-Archives/processus-contra-templarios-2

Cardinals feared for their lives. Their arms were easily twisted to select Philip's boyhood friend to become Pope Clement V in 1305. In 1309, under imperial pressure, Clement moved his offices to the comfort of Avignon. Here the clergy hierarchy were kept by the King in the lap of luxury. This 68-year period is called by historians the "Babylonian Captivity of the Papacy."[8] From 1309 to 1376 seven successive popes would reside in opulence there. By the end of the fourteenth century, there would be rival Popes!

On January 17, 1377 Pope Gregory XI returned the Papal residency to Rome. But with his death in 1378, the Church once again divided. At this time, nearly all of the cardinals were sons from the powerful families in and around Rome. Their family squabbles and rivalries spilled into the workings of the Church cardinals! This split has been called the Western Schism. One group returned to Avignon while the other remained in Rome. And both groups selected their own popes.

---

[8] Adrian Hastings, Alistair Mason and Hugh S. Pyper, *The Oxford Companion to Christian Thought*, Oxford University Press, 2000,

"In the period of the [Western] Schism, the power struggle in the papacy became a battlefield of the major powers, with France supporting the Pope in Avignon and its rival, England, supporting the Pope in Rome. At the end of the century, still in the state of schism, the papacy had lost most of its direct political power while the nation states of France and England had established themselves as two of the main national powers in Europe."[9]

Well-intentioned councils met to resolve the differences. After unsuccessfully attempting to get these two Popes to meet and resolve things, a council was held without them at Pisa. This council resolved to depose both Popes in absentia, and to elect a new Pope, a third Pope. This was Alexander V who would be pope for only 10 months. Now there were three Popes at the same time: Gregory XII, Benedict XIII, and Alexander V. "In 1410 Alexander sent to Archbishop Zbynek of Prague a bull which ordered the burning of Wycliffe's heretical works [translations of the Bible from Latin to a common language]. Alexander died mysteriously, some

---

9 https://en.wikipedia.org/wiki/Avignon_Papacy#cite_ref-2 accessed 14Aug2018

professing—though without proof—that he was poisoned by his successor, the [so-called] antipope John XXIII."[10]

This schism finally came to an end when this new third Pope, John XXIII, convened the Council of Constance (1414 – 1417) at which he magnanimously offered to resign if the council could agree on a new Pope. A second of the three Popes, Roman Pope Gregory XII also supported the Council and offered as well to step down if an agreeable new Pope could be elected. But the Avignon Pope, Benedict XIII, refused. Thus, to end this schism, the Council excommunicated him. Typically, France would have sided with whoever was in Avignon. But, fortunately for the Church, Benedict XIII was hugely unpopular. Thus, in 1417, only thirty-five years before Leonardo da Vinci would be born, the Western Schism came to an end. Oddone Colonna, a Pisan cardinal, was selected as the new Pope for all Roman Catholics. As Pope, he took on the new name Martin V and subsequently restored the Papal States in Rome.

---

[10] Encyclopedia Brittanica, https://www.britannica.com/biography/Alexander-V, accessed 22Apr2020

The Great Schism and the Western Schism

Three hundred years earlier, in 1054, the Church of Rome had split with the Church of Constantinople with mutual excommunications. A long simmering feud since Constantine had moved the capital city of the Roman Empire from Rome to Constantinople boiled over in 1054.

By the fifth century, Rome was no longer the Rome of the glory years of the Roman Empire. In 410, it was sacked by Visigoths from the North. In 455, it suffered a much more destructive attack by another Gothic tribe, the Vandals, who raided from their new kingdom in Tunisia. A century later Rome suffered extensive damage when it was caught in the middle of 20-year struggle between the Ostrogoths and the Byzantine Empire. During this sixth century war, it changed hands several times. At one point it was emptied of all inhabitants. It would return as a Papal power late in the eighth century through the protection of the Holy Roman Empire under Charlemagne whose father, Pepin, had been deceived by Pope Stephen with a forged document now called The Donation of

Constantine.[11] As a city-state, the Vatican grew in power and influence during the ninth and tenth centuries.

By 1054, Rome had reasserted itself as a power, albeit religious, throughout the Mediterranean area. As Constantinople buffered Rome from the east while France safely held the western and northern fronts, Rome grew wealthy. Early "Eleventh century Rome was a medieval city like no other. Rich Romans lived in homes built into classical ruins— abandoned theaters, stadiums and long dry baths. The Colosseum was the city's largest housing complex."[12]

In the aftermath of the Great Schism, the Fourth Crusade would sack Constantinople in 1204. Because insufficient funds existed for

---

[11] "The *Donation of Constantine* (Latin: Donatio Constantini) is a forged Roman imperial decree (Diplom) by which the fourth century emperor Constantine the Great supposedly transferred authority over Rome and the western part of the Roman Empire to the Pope. Composed probably in the eighth century, it was used, especially in the thirteenth century, in support of claims of political authority by the papacy." - https://en.wikipedia.org/wiki/Donation_of_Constantine#

[12] Matthew Kneale, *Rome: A History in Seven Sackings*, Simon & Schuster, 2018

the crusade, the Doge of Venice, Enrico Dandolo, reasoned that the army could plunder there, sell the stolen goods and relics to their churches in the West to raise sufficient funds to pay for the crusade and its mercenary army and supplies. Plundered were countless precious jewels, ornaments, and relics from Hagia Sophia and possibly what is known today as the Shroud of Turin. The Byzantine Empire was then divided up among some of the leaders of this Fourth Crusader. Baldwin of Flanders was crowned as Emperor Baldwin I.

The new Latin rulers were disliked by their Greek-speaking populace. Some former Byzantine aristocrats managed to establish a number of small independent states. From these strongholds, they would eventually recapture Constantinople in 1261 and restore its Patriarch. But the restored Byzantine Empire was so weakened it would eventually fall to the Ottoman Sultanate in the 1453. Although military help from the West was sought by the East, agreeable terms could never be reached. One such mission convened the Council of Florence in 1438. It brought to Florence the scholar, Gemistus Plethon, whom I call the Catalyst for the Renaissance. No doubt the Renaissance would never have happened without his lectures and a trunk full of texts that inspired Cosimo de Medici to found a Platonic Academy in Florence.

2. Knowledge Returns, Steps to the Reformation

The Council of Constance was convened in 1414 to resolve the issue of three popes. In order to find common ground, it first dealt with more uniting matters, namely condemning new heresies! The bishops dealt first with one of their own invited reformers, Jan Huss.

As a prominent voice in the argument for ecclesiastical reform, Johannes or Jan Huss had agreed to attend but only with the guarantee of safe passage. He knew many dogmatists of the Church viewed him as a rebel and some wanted him to be at least excommunicated or, preferably, to have him be declared a heretic. Such a declaration meant death. With assurances of safety from Emperor Sigismund, Huss attended. But the Council, nonetheless, declared him a heretic and sentenced him to be burned at the stake in July 1415.

Huss' colleague, Jerome of Prague, arrived late to Constance. He too was declared to be a heretic and he too was burnt. To ensure that there were no relics for supporters, the council had the ashes of the two scattered in the Rhine. Now feeling unity, the Council then ordered that the body of John Wycliffe (1320s – 1384) be dug up, burnt, and also dumped into a river. Wycliffe's main offense was that he had translated the New Testament from Latin into English.

Figure 4 Pope, Bishops, and the Beast of the Apocalypse, illustration from Jenske Codex

The illustration here shows why the populace felt disgusted about these horrific acts by Church delegates at the Council of Constance. Illustrators depicted the Council members as being embraced by the beast of the Apocalypse. The brutality done to these respected men, whose deaths barely preceded that of Leonardo da Vinci, would gestate and eventually give birth to the Protestant Reformation[13] soon after Leonardo's death.

The Hussite or Bohemian Rebellion

When news of Huss's treatment and death at the Council reached his hometown of Prague, it set off a rebellion against the Church. Huss' successor as preacher declared four principles for reform. The Reformation in eastern Europe thus began in 1415 and built momentum over the next 200 years. This Reformation would lead to the first national European church that separated from Roman authority.

Birthing the Protestant Reformation

Because the Church in Rome was perceived as corrupt, by 1438, it had little sway to move any monarch, especially when it requested military

---

[13] Emily Michael, "John Wyclif on Body and Mind", Journal of the History of Ideas, 2003, p. 343

forces to help defend Christianity in Constantinople. Echoes of voices such as John Wycliffe (1330 – 1384) who had called for an end to an increasingly imperialized papacy grew louder. Wycliffe's later works such as the *Trialogus, Dialogus,* and *Opus Evangelicum,* compared the papacy with its monks to a monarch using its soldiers to quell its growing opposition.[14] Naturally, his books were seen by the bishops as an attack on the papacy itself.[15] All of Wycliffe's works would be deemed to be heretical.

When Martin Luther posted his Ninety-five Theses in 1517, Leonardo da Vinci was nearing the end of his life living in France. His Europe was feeling the groundswell leading to the Protestant Reformation.

Historians credit Henry VIII (1491 – 1547) with commencing the English Reformation when he separated the Church of England from papal authority. Once a devout Catholic, Henry became resentful and angry when his request in 1527 to annul his marriage to Catherine of

---

[14] Akim Maseko, Church Schism and Corruption: Book 3, 2008

[15] Rudolph Buddensieg. *John Wiclif's Polemical works in Latin*, Vol.2, The Wyclif Society, 1883

Aragon was denied. Catherine was unable to procreate a boy to succeed Henry. Catherine was well connected. She was the widow of Henry's brother, Arthur, the daughter of Ferdinand and Isabella of Spain, and the aunt of Holy Roman Emperor Charles V. Just months earlier, Charles' imperial troops of the Holy Roman Empire had attacked and destroyed Rome. Pope Clement VII had fled through a secret tunnel. He took shelter in the Castel Sant'Angelo.

Once against the Protestant Reformation, Henry saw political opportunity. With the ghost of John Wycliffe "approving," Parliament passed legislation between 1532 and 1534 that declared Henry to be the "Supreme Head on earth of the [new] Church of England". Further, the legislation eliminated the Pope's "soldiers" by dissolving all Catholic convents and monasteries in England. With his new moral authority, Henry would find cause to divorce and marry five more times. The Pope in Rome, Clement VII, who had warned Henry of excommunication should he divorce Catherina and remarry, naturally had to follow through on his threat.

The Protestant Reformation continued throughout sixteenth century Europe lasting until the end of the vicious Thirty Years' War in 1648. Accusations and declarations of heresy were plentiful during this brutal period.

The New Renaissance Philosophy: Humanism

Not only was the power of the Church waning, but its theology was also under attack. Although materialism was entrenched by the start of the Renaissance, Humanism[16] was on the rise. With the Church's authority undermined, boldness to challenge its dogma arose. The battle of Knowledge versus Faith once fought by Saint Augustine now reemerged as the struggle between knowing and blind faith. This battle was especially clear in the struggles over translations of the bible as mentioned above. This time, the Church argued that the jewels of spirit should not be tarnished in the hands of the common man. It

[16] "Humanism is a philosophical and ethical stance that emphasizes the value and agency of human beings, individually and collectively, and generally prefers critical thinking and evidence (rationalism and empiricism) over acceptance of dogma or superstition" from https://en.wikipedia.org/wiki/Humanism accessed 14Aug2018

did not notice the irony that such a position was eerily similar to the heretical one the Gnostics had taken 1300 years earlier.

The Inquisition allowed the Church to cling to religious power. Being declared a heretic likely meant death, before, during, and after the Renaissance. Giordano Bruno, 1548 – 1600, oddly a Dominican friar[17] but also a philosopher, a mathematician, a poet, an astrologer and an astronomer, was burned at the stake on February 17, 1600. His death sentence came because he proposed that the Sun was just another star moving in space and the universe contained an infinite number of inhabited worlds populated by other intelligent beings.

Similarly, Galileo Galilei, 1564 – 1642, the "father of modern science,"[18] was tried for his view that the earth was not the center of the universe. A Roman Inquisition, in 1615, concluded that heliocentrism was "foolish and absurd in philosophy, and formally heretical since it explicitly contradicts in many places

---

[17] The Dominicans were typically the monks who held court for Inquisitions.
[18] Isaac Disraeli, *Curiosities of Literature*, W. Pearson & Company, p. 371, 1835

the sense of Holy Scripture."[19] Galileo later defended his views in *Dialogue Concerning the Two Chief World Systems* (1632). Until this point, the Jesuits, had supported Galileo, but now they turned against him as his book appeared to attack Pope Urban VIII. All Jesuits take an oath to support the Pope in all situations. Galileo was tried in 1633 by an Inquisition that found his work to be heretical and they forced him to recant. Unlike Bruno, his life was spared but he had to spend the last nine years of his life under house arrest. The Church banned Galileo's works until 1718.

Even Italian scientist, Francesco Redi, was looked upon by seventeenth century scientists as a dangerous heretic because he asserted that the lower animals reproduced themselves. Science at that time believed that worms, insects, and most fish originated from inanimate mud. Redi worked from the assumption that life must originate from the living. What he asserted would become accepted as true two centuries later. He barely escaped the martyr's death of Giordano Bruno.

---

[19] Maurice Finocchiaro, *Defending Copernicus and Galileo: Critical Reasoning in the two Affairs*, Springer, 2010

Platonic Academy of Florence

History and theology through the eyes of Leonardo da Vinci was to be our point of departure. Thus, it is fitting to describe the Platonic Academy in Florence which became the center of learning in Europe in the fifteenth century. Biographer John Addington Symonds places Michelangelo Buonarroti as a student of the Platonic Academy.[20] Clearly, Leonardo, as another brilliant student belonging to the prior generation of students in Verrocchio's art school, would also have participated. What, besides Neoplatonism, would one be exposed to within this academy? Texts on Hermetic Magic, Greek philosophies, and esoteric Early Christian writings from George Gemistus Plethon and others were central for the content of this academy.

The Academy itself was forced to dissolve when both its leading teachers, Poliziano and Mirandola, were poisoned in 1494.[21] The Platonic Academy's environment would have pulsed with the theological and scientific controversies of the day as well as those of

---

[20] John A. Symonds, *The Life of Michelangelo*, Capricorn Books, pp. 405-408, 1962

[21] Malcolm Moore, "Medici philosopher's mysterious death is solved," The Daily Telegraph. London. 7Feb2008

prior centuries. Several groups sought to bring this academy, as a threat to Church dogma, to a close.

We will now explore some of this Christian history from Plato up to the Renaissance and its Platonic Academy of Florence. We also know that the Florentine artists were inspired to relate Greek mythologies to Christianity. Within this academy, these myths were seen as a kind of prophecy for what was to come with Christianity. One was led back to the golden years of Greece when its culture was derived from its Mystery Centers.

In the larger picture of human evolution, we can follow a path of transition from the tribe to the city-state to the citizen to the individual. During this transition, the thinking experience went from "it thinks in me" to "I think." This was also the transition from being a group member to being an ego. This would be a transition that brought forth individual Freedom and with it, Egoism. Such a change meant that what lived in the Mystery Centers and how it operated would naturally become corrupted by the rising egoism. As a consequence, its leaders had to allow them to fade away.

3. Christianity's Philosophical Foundations

The Jewish writer Philo was the Immanuel Kant of the eastern Mediterranean region at the time when Christianity entered the world. Within this Hellenistic world, to be taken seriously, a true philosopher needed to show how the construction of his own self happened according to their philosophy. Borrowing from Stoic doctrine, Philo elaborated on the concept of the Logos, the meaning of life. He concluded that God's consciousness is The Logos. Because humanity and the world were created through this Logos, then the human being shares the same spiritual nature with God. But God is perfect in his nature while mankind is perfectible. And so, even though Mankind is created in the image of God, full knowledge of Him is an imponderable.

In the *Probus 20,* Philo reasons that only he who has no other master than God is free.[22] Such a perspective on Freedom would not have been possible 800 years earlier. Thus, a person seeking audience with God, had to first attain freedom by inner work to regulate one's

---

[22] J. H. A. Hart, *The Jewish Quarterly Review,* Original Series 17, pp. 731-737

own nature, to control one's passions and emotions, and to eliminate any gap between theory and practice thereby attain human perfection. We'll see this theme of becoming a *perfect* arising again and again within Christian streams.

Philosophy as the Servant of Revelation

It is difficult for people today to grasp the importance that both philosophy and theology had for the Hellenistic world of the first century. Few people today find such questions and discussions to be of any interest and certainly of much less interest than politics, or celebrity gossip, or new technological gadgets. The here-and-now is what matters today. Separated from religion, philosophy, and art, science today acts as our sole guide. But this was not true in the first century. Formerly, the ancient mysteries had served as the guide for their respective ethnic group. But by the time of Aristotle (384 – 322 BC), these mystery centers were fading and failing. For many first century philosophers like Philo of Alexandria (25 BC – 50 AD), the former Temple initiations that had taken place secretly within the Holy of the Holies, could now take place within the inner sanctuary of the human soul.

Philo

Philo's path was a path of knowledge akin to that of the great philosophers Pythagoras and Plato. While not labeled a Gnostic, we find very similar themes in Philo (Gnosticism was a path of knowledge leading to an experience of God. It will be described later). In the prologue (chapter 1) of John's Gospel we find mention of Darkness as a conscious being. "Life is the Light of Man(kind). And this Light [Gnostics use the term divine spark] shines into the Darkness and the Darkness has comprehended it not."[23] This prologue aligns with Philo's philosophy.

Philo argued that only way to have real existence was to admit that one is nothing without the help of God. Only with union with God was one free. Only through striving to reach the consciousness of the mind of God, i.e., the Logos, could one achieve an experience of God.

Philo, a Jewish philosopher, described the concept of a Logos as the mediator between the earthly world of the senses and God's imponderable heavenly world. One can approach God, but only through the Logos.

---

[23] John 1:4

Interestingly, John's Gospel[24] builds upon this Logos-philosophy of Philo, "No one comes to the Father except through me [the Logos]."[25]

Before Philo, Platonism was the dominant philosophy of the Hellenistic world from Alexandria to Athens. This would be followed early in the third century with Neoplatonism whose center in Alexandria, Egypt provided rich soil for three generations of Neoplatonic philosophers.

Body, Soul, and Spirit

We cannot understand these Greek and first century philosophers without also understanding the concepts of body (soma), soul (psyche), and spirit (pneuma). For them, as for Shakespeare, the earth is the stage for the great cosmic drama.[26] On this stage our soul acts. For Philo, all sacred texts, e.g., those of Moses, contained truths on multiple levels. Allegorical truths were for him those that are

---

[24] John 1:1, "In the Beginning the Logos was, And the Logos was with God."

[25] John 14:6 "I am the way, the truth, and the life: no man cometh unto the Father, but by me." KJV

[26] William Shakespeare, *As You Like It*, spoken by Jacques, "All the world's a stage. And all the men and women merely players; They have their exits and their entrances; And one man in his time plays many parts, His acts being seven ages."

not necessarily true on the physical level but are truths on a higher level. These allegories described the knowledge path that the soul must follow for reunion with God. This path leads to a soul-level understanding of the Logos. Then the soul can resound with the Logos within.

The Prominent Philosophers of Florence's Platonic Academy

The significant influence of the following additional three philosophers on the Hellenistic world and on the Early Christians should not be underestimated. As this chapter progresses, we will see their concepts woven into the fabric of Early Christianity. Although Christianity brought new concepts, they had to be understood first through the prevailing philosophies. As we shall see, philosophy and theology lost their boundary. From the start of the Ecumenical Councils into the seventeenth century, the Roman Church felt it to be its obligation to ensure the right faith prevailed. At the start of the Renaissance, in the mid-fifteenth century, Florence was gifted with texts and lecturers from the East that rebirthed Greek philosophy and Early Christian writings enabling students such as Leonardo da

Vinci to learn of these philosophies and theologies within Florence's Platonic Academy.

Plato

Plato (424-327 BC) was one of the greatest of all philosophers. His works shaped the Hellenistic period. For what we will need to grasp Plato's contribution to the theme for this chapter, the following quotes will suffice. In the first quote, we hear of initiations within the Mysteries as well as the concept of becoming perfected, a *Perfect*.

> *"Only a philosopher's mind grows wings, since its memory always keeps it as close as possible to those realities by being close to which the gods are divine. A man who uses reminders of these things correctly is always at the highest, most perfect level of initiation, and he is the only one who is perfect as perfect can be. He stands outside human concerns and draws close to the divine; ordinary people think he is disturbed and rebuke him for this,*

unaware that he is possessed by god."[27]

Christian-Gnostic philosophy of the first century also spoke of working upon oneself in this way.

The next quote, from a book by Crystal Addey, gives an historian's perspective of Plato's relationship to the ancient Mysteries.

"Plato frequently employs mystery cult terminology and imagery to describe the philosophical vision and contemplation of the Forms (Ideals). For instance, in the Phaedo, Socrates compares philosophers to those who have been purified and initiated, referring to initiatory rites in general. In the Symposium, Plato uses the traditional language of the Festival of the greater mysteries at Eleusis to describe

---

[27] Plato, *Phaedrus* (a different book than *Phaedo*), translation by Benjamin Jowett, MIT

the philosopher's contemplation of the Forms."[28]

Plato, it appears, was an initiate of the Mysteries and likely would have initiated his most brilliant student Aristotle. Plato described the purpose of the Mysteries:

> *"The ultimate design of the Mysteries ... was to lead us back to the principles from which we descended, ... a perfect enjoyment of the spiritually good."*[29]

As an initiate, Plato wrote about his own spiritual experiences.

> *"Of the heaven which is above the heavens, what earthly poet ever did or ever will sing worthily? It is such as I will describe; for I must dare to speak the truth, when truth is my theme. There abides the very being with which true*

---

[28] Crystal Addey, *Divination and Theurgy in Neoplatonism: Oracles of the Gods*, Routledge, 2014

[29] Plato, Phaedo, from Thomas Taylor, *The Eleusinian and Bacchic Mysteries*, Kessinger Publ, 2010

knowledge is concerned; the colorless, formless, intangible essence, visible only to mind, the pilot of the soul. The divine intelligence, being nurtured upon mind and pure knowledge, and the intelligence of every soul which is capable of receiving the food proper to it, rejoices at beholding reality, and once more gazing upon truth, is replenished and made glad, until the revolution of the worlds brings her round again to the same place. In the revolution she beholds justice, and temperance, and knowledge absolute, not in the form of generation or of relation, which men call existence, but knowledge absolute in existence absolute; and beholding the other true existences in like manner, and feasting upon them, she passes down into the interior of the heavens and returns home."[30]

In his *Dialogue on the Immortality of the Soul,* Plato mentions purification.

> *"Our mysteries had a very real meaning: he that has been purified and initiated shall dwell with the gods"*[31]

He goes on to describe an initiation experience with the death of Socrates as experienced by his character Phaedo:

> *"Nothing gives me more pleasure than recalling the memory of Socrates, either by talking myself or by listening to someone else. For my part, I had strange emotions when I was there. For I was not filled with pity as I might naturally be when present at the death of a friend; since he seemed to me to be happy, both in his bearing and his words. He was meeting death so fearlessly*

---

[30] Plato, *Phaedrus,* translation by Benjamin Jowett, MIT

[31] Plato, *Phaedo*, F.J. Church translation

and nobly. And so, I thought that even in going to the abode of the dead he was not going without the protection of the gods, and that when he arrived there it would be well with him, if it ever was well with anyone. And for this reason, I was not at all filled with pity, as might seem natural when I was present at a scene of mourning; nor on the other hand did I feel pleasure, as was our custom when we were occupied with philosophy — although our talk was of philosophy — but a very strange feeling came over me, an unaccustomed mixture of pleasure and of pain together, when I thought that Socrates was presently to die."[32]

At the Platonic Academy in Florence, all students would have heard about Plato's "Dialogue on Love" contained within his book

[32] Plato, *Phaedo*, 58 D-E, translation by E. A. Frommer.

Symposium. Here love is described as the herald of wisdom. Why would a soul seek wisdom? The soul must contain a longing that draws it towards the divine. For Plato, that which was unconscious when raised into consciousness brings supreme joy. Rudolf Steiner describes this relationship of wisdom, love, and the logos.

In the Symposium, people of the most varied status, possessing the most varied views on life, all spoke of love. This included the man in the street, the politician, the scientist, the poet of comedy, and the serious poet. Each had his or her own conception of love determined by how that one had experienced life. How they expressed themselves revealed the development state of their daemon.

Through love one being is drawn to another. For Plato, divine unity was diffused into the manifold variety of things. Through love, these created things strove towards oneness and harmony. As such, love must be a divine quality. And every human was capable of understanding it. But this could happen only insofar as one had partaken of this divine quality. Thus, wisdom, the Eternal Word, must be the Son of the Eternal Creator. And love must have a maternal relationship with this Logos.

Socrates then entered this discussion on love. He considered love from the viewpoint of a thinker. For him God was perfect, possessing beauty and goodness. Eros, love, was no god for him. Love was something that led one to God. Eros, thus, was the longing for beauty and goodness. Eros stands between the human and God. He is a daemon, a mediator between the earthly and the divine.

What makes this passage so significant is that Socrates claimed he was not speaking from his own philosophy but was recounting a revelation about it that he received from a wise woman! The priestess Diotima had awakened in Socrates this daemon. She had initiated him.

Who was this wise woman? We must seek this wise woman in the soul of Socrates himself. There must, however, be a basis which allows what brings the daemon to birth in the soul to appear as a being in external reality. This force cannot work in the same way as the forces we can observe in the soul as belonging to it and at home with it. We see that it is the force of the soul before it has received wisdom, which Socrates represents as the "wise woman." It is the maternal principle which gives birth to the Son of God, Wisdom, the Logos.

The unconscious force of the soul is presented as a feminine element, which allows the divine to enter consciousness. The soul which as yet lacks wisdom is the mother of what leads to the divine. This leads us to an important idea of mysticism. The soul is recognized as the mother of the divine. With the inevitability of a natural force, it unconsciously leads one toward the divine. — This point throws light on the conception held in the Mysteries regarding Greek mythology. The world of the gods is born in the soul.

Man regards as his gods what he himself creates in the form of pictures. But he must progress to another idea. He must transform into pictures of the gods the divine force present in himself which is active before the creation of these pictures of the gods. The mother of the divine appears behind the divine, and this is none other than the original force in the human soul. Man places goddesses beside his gods.[33]

Now, when we take up the myth of Dionysus, we can understand it in the light of the above. Who was Dionysus? He was the son of Zeus, the leader of the gods, with a mortal, a woman named Semele. Semele was struck by Zeus' lightning. As she lay dying, Zeus tore the premature infant from her and inserts the unborn child into his thigh. Later, when fully gestated, Zeus gave birth to Dionysus. But Hera, wife of Zeus and mother of the gods, was jealous. She incited the Titans to rise up against Dionysus. They dismember him.[34] But Pallas Athene saved the boy's still beating

---

[33] Rudolf Steiner, *Christianity as Mystical Fact*, translated by Anthroposophic Press, 2nd edition, 1973. The German word "mensch" is genderless but in translating to English "man" was used in this 1973 translation.

[34] Compare this Greek myth to the Egyptian myth of Osiris who is dismembered.

heart and took it to Zeus who thus begat this son for the second time!

This myth describes a process which takes place in the depths of the human soul. Dionysus was the son of an immortal with a mortal mother as was Jesus. He was killed yet was born again through the forces of love, expressed as the still-beating heart. This too seems to prophesize the future Christian theology.

How does the birth of the divine in the human soul come about? Whenever the soul begins to long for its spiritual nature, the everyday consciousness becomes stirred to stop this "foolery". In a form of jealousy, it incites one's lower nature, that is, one's Titans to put an end to this longing. The immature divine child within, is, in this sense, dismembered by these inner Titans. This dismembered wholeness now scattered in one's intellect by reductionistic, materialistic science. It can, with the higher wisdom of Zeus, be brought to rebirth as the Son of Man. To this born-again son, the Greeks gave the mythical name Dionysus. We see how the Renaissance artists were inspired to explore how Greek mythology may be related to Christianity.

Thus, out of science, out of the dismembered divine force in man, is born the harmonizing wisdom, which is the Logos, the son of God and of a mortal mother, who is the transitory soul of man striving unconsciously for the divine. We are far from the spiritual reality represented in all this as long as we see in it only a mere process of the soul and take it as a picture of this process. In this spiritual reality the soul does not merely experience something within itself; it is completely disconnected from itself and participates in a cosmic process which in truth takes place outside itself and not within it.[35]

Plutarch

Better known as a biographer, Plutarch's (45 – 120) philosophical writings also played a significant role in what is called the Middle

---

[35] IBID, R. Steiner, CAMF.

Platonic era. The founding fathers of America studied Plutarch's strong stance on the freedom of will and his view on the immortality of the soul, or at least an aspect of the soul.[36] Plutarch's philosophy described God as a transcendent being whose on-going creative thoughts are carried out by a hierarchy of divine beings. Such a hierarchy was common. Thus, lesser divine beings acted as intermediaries within their realm. For Plutarch, these lesser divine beings are the gods that appear in pagan myths. In creating the physical world, God transformed spirit into matter so that evil could have a role in human evolution. Gnosticism (discussed later) would claim that a Demiurge transformed spirit into matter belonging to the darkness, thereby establishing a duality into which Mankind was placed.

Plutarch wrote that the world itself had a dual soul, one divine and one that succumbs to evil but still can be transformed. Plutarch, writing to his wife on the death of their daughter, says, *"because of those sacred and faithful*

---

[36] Alexander Hamilton and Cotton Mather often quoted Plutarch. Of his biographies, Ralph Waldo Emerson called *Lives* "a bible for heroes." The Transcendentalists studied his *Moralia.*

promises given in the mysteries...we hold it firmly for an undoubted truth that our soul is incorruptible and immortal. Let us behave ourselves accordingly." He then added, "When a man dies, he is like those who are initiated into the mysteries. Our whole life is a journey by tortuous ways without outlet. At the moment of quitting, it come terrors, shuddering fear, amazement. Then a light that moves to meet you, pure meadows that receive you, songs and dances and holy apparitions"[37]

Plotinus

The next great philosopher of the region, Plotinus (204 – 269), extended the Neoplatonic philosophy found in Philo. That which Plato calls the world of ideas was for Plotinus both a spiritual and an intellectual world. The boundary of the spiritual world was human concepts.

Plotinus wrote, *"as the sun's rays illuminate a dark cloud and make it golden, so does the soul, on entering the body of the world encircled by the sky, give it life and*

---

37 http://penelope.uchicago.edu/Thayer/E/Roman/Texts/Plutarch/Moralia/Consolatio_ad_uxorem*.html

immortality."[38] Keep this in mind for when we examine the canons of the Eighth Ecumenical Council.

Plotinus claimed that for inner initiation to take place within the soul,

> *"We must enter deep into ourselves, and, leaving behind the objects of corporeal sight, no longer look back after any of the accustomed spectacles of sense. For, it is necessary that whoever beholds this beauty, should withdraw his view from the fairest corporeal forms; and, convinced that these are nothing more than images, vestiges and shadows of beauty, should eagerly soar to the fair original from which they are derived."*[39]

While Neoplatonism sought the Logos in the spiritual realm, Early Christianity believed the Logos had become flesh. Whereas the Logos

---

[38] Richard Ward, *The Life of Henry More, Parts 1 & 2*, Springer Science, 2000

[39] Plotinus, "An Essay on the Beautiful", translated into English by Thomas Taylor, 1917

once had been found on a path of Knowledge in the Ancient Mysteries, now, following Easter, the Logos could be sought also in the physical life. Neoplatonism and Early Christianity shared much in their philosophical and mystical perspectives.

A mere hundred years later, Augustine would study Plotinus and the other Neoplatonists. But during that century, initiation into the spiritual world had ceased. Augustine could no longer travel in this world of ideas to where one could experience a spiritual world. Despite attempts at initiation, he could not behold a spiritual world. He could learn about a spiritual world living within a world of ideas only from others but not from his own experience. Materialism had closed the door by the fourth century to the spiritual world.

A thousand years later, within the walls of Florence's Platonic Academy, Leonardo learned about these philosophers and their philosophies. Leonardo also learned how these philosophies had become heresies as nascent Christianity evolved along with a world perspective increasingly dominated by Materialism.

Hellenistic Philosophy of the Earth and its Elements

The following passage from *The Life of Apollonius of Tyana* by Philostratus illustrates the Greek concepts for the four elements and above them an etheric realm. The idea that light travels as an ether would persist into the start of the twentieth century.

> *"And they allowed Apollonius to ask questions, and he asked them of what they thought the cosmos was composed, but they replied, "Of elements."*
>
> *"Are there then four?" he asked.*
>
> *"Not four," said Larchas, "but five."*
>
> *"And how can there be a fifth," said Apollonius, "alongside of water and air and earth and fire?"*
>
> *"There is the aether," replied the other, "which we must regard as the stuff of which gods are made, for just as all mortal creatures inhale the air, so do immortal and divine natures inhale the aether."*

"Am I," said Appollonius, "to regard the universe as a living creature?"

"Yes," said the other.[40]

The sciences in Hellenistic times studied the four elements of the earth. Science today calls these the four states of matter. To the Greek, wind was much more than fast moving air particles. Its word, pneuma, also meant spirit. For the Greek, these were the same, but they saw matter as an expression of the spirit. We find this philosophy embedded in many Early Christian writings such as the Gospel of Philip:

What is harvested in the world is
composed of four elements:
earth, water, wind, and light. [earth,
water, air, and fire in Greek model]
What God harvests is also composed of
four elements:
Pistis [faith], Elpis [hope], Agape [spiritual
love], and Gnosis [contemplation].
Our earth is faith, for she gives us roots.
Water is our hope, for it slakes our thirst.

---

[40] *The Life of Apollonius of Tyana*, by Philostratus, 220AD, tells the story of Apollonius of Tyana (c. 15 – c. 100 AD) who was a Pythagorean philosopher and teacher

Wind [pneuma] is the love [agape]
through which we grow.
And light is the contemplation [gnosis]
through which we ripen.[41]

Key Points from Philosophical Foundations

Many scholars such as Rudolf Bultmann have concluded that Christianity had its roots in these Hellenistic philosophies as well as Gnosticism (discussed later).[42] Of the four Gospels, John's has the closest ties to Philo with its Logos concept and to Gnosticism with its concept of Darkness as a being.

In the Beginning the Logos was, and the Logos was with God.

[A] God the Logos was. This oneness with God was in the Beginning.

---

[41] *The Gospel of Philip*, translated by Jean-Yves Leloup, Inner Traditions, 2004

[42] Rudolf Bultmann, *The Gospel of John: A Commentary*, Westminster John Knox Press, 1971; *Primitive Christianity: In Its Contemporary Setting*, Thames & Hudson, 1983; and *Theology of the New Testament*, Baylor University Press, 2007

All things emerged through Him. Not one thing has emerged that emerged without Him.

In Him is Life. Life is the Light of Mankind. This Light shines in the Darkness and the Darkness has not comprehended it.[43]

Of particular interest to us here is the concept God espoused in this passage. Many theological debates were waged over the concept of the Trinity of God, some resulted in bloodshed by those labeled “heretics”. Simply, the Christian concept of the Trinity blended together as one Godhead: The Father, the Son, and the Holy Spirit. For some theologians, this verse above brings a different concept of Trinity. They find that the missing definitive article τὸν (ton) before Θεὸς (theos) in line 2 above renders that sentence as “a God” rather than “the God”. Jehovah Witnesses, for example, ascribe to this understanding.

---

[43] John 1:1-4, my translation based on the interlinear: https://biblehub.com/interlinear/john/1.htm

Early Christians had varied views about the Trinity. Some reasoned that since Stephen could see Christ standing at the right hand of the Father (Acts 7:55-56) and since Christ himself prayed to His Father and called the Father greater than he himself (John 14:28), and that the Father would send the Holy Spirit, that these three were different Gods. Recall the earlier mention of a heavenly hierarchy of nine levels. Some believed that the Christ had become one with the Logos before the beginning of Earth evolution, and then, during earth evolution, He descended through the hierarchies becoming, as he went, a 'lesser' god until he became a human. Some saw Christ as one of the Gods of the Elohim or Exusiai rank who had become one with the Logos before Earth's evolution. For most Early Christians, this not-the-Father God was 'born' into the body of Jesus of Nazareth at the baptism. During the ensuing three years, this Christ would say, "my hour has not yet come"[44] until he had fully become one with this human body. Then the great sacrifice, the willing death of a God on Golgotha, could take

[44] See John 2:4, 7:6, 7:30, and 8:20. In John 12:23 Jesus says, "The hour has come for the Son of Man to be glorified."

place. This theological view would become seen as heretical and thus banned.

Lastly, we need to examine the theological and philosophical issue of the human soul. In these key philosophers we find the concept that not only do they speak of a human soul but also of a world soul. Both souls have two aspects: a heavenly and an earthly aspect. If one drew these aspects as a triangle, one would draw two triangles that would make a six-pointed star.

As theology evolved from the fourth century to the ninth, confusion entered. Some reasoned that humans have but one soul while others claimed that each human had two different souls: one concerned with the earthly and one with the heavenly. As this debate emerged, the concept of the human spirit, pneuma, faded away as materialism predominated. This debate would eventually be settled at the Eighth Ecumenical Council of 869 CE. There it was decreed that the human being consists of one body and only one soul and nothing else. The concept of a heavenly soul in addition to an earthly soul became a heresy as did any mention of a human spirit. Coincidentally, at this time the eucharist was altered so that the congregation received only the bread while the wine was reserved for the clergy. The wine had been the representative of the human spirit. Then began the Troubadours and their stories sung about the lost Holy Grail.

The Fate of Knowledge from Plato to the Renaissance

The Platonic Academy in Florence acted as an inspiration for the subjects of Renaissance art. We have examined some of the content of the Greek philosophers, the Neoplatonists, and the Ancient Mysteries in order to see how different this content was from the contemporary theological and philosophical content of the pre-Renaissance that had been largely controlled by Catholicism. We will see how Charlemagne had been given a gift of teachers from the court of Harun al-Rashid whose metaphysics led to a flowering of a school at Chartres that bloomed first with Platonic philosophy and later with an Aristotelianism base. Oddly, this knowledge grew mainly within the monasteries of the Catholic Church.

The dry wood was ready for the philosophical fire when Plethon arrived in 1438 for the Council of Florence. Gemistus Plethon had joined the Byzantium delegation that hoped to mend the Great Schism of 1054 when the Pope and the Patriarch excommunicated each other (more on this later). Plethon's lectures in Florence ignited the enthusiasm for this knowledge from the East. Although admittedly a pagan and not an affirmed Christian, Plethon's lectures made it obvious that the Greek Mysteries and philosophers had an expectation of the coming of Christianity. With what flowed from the Platonic Academy, Renaissance artists were inspired to explore the connection Christianity had with the ancient Mysteries and mythologies. But, with an active Inquisition still endangering Knowledge explorers, those who were able would hide their discoveries within their art.

This chapter will examine this theme with a focus on the transition period from Hellenism, based as it was on the ancient Mysteries, to Christianity. We will see how mysticism was originally an integrated part of Early Christianity. We will see how these ancient streams flowed and mixed with the nascent Christianity until fourth century Christian leaders called for a complete break with this past. We will explore how mysticism was rooted out as a heresy. As we study this, let us carry the question: did awareness of its brutal repression cause a resentment towards the Church especially in those of the forefront of Knowledge such as Leonardo da Vinci?

Aristotle and Alexander as Great Initiates

Aristotle (384–322 BC) wrote the *Secret of Secrets* to his pupil, Alexander the Great (356-320 BC), offering it as a royal guidebook in the proper art of government and personal royal conduct. It taught of the moral basis of one as a royal ruler and covered, from this foundation, the sciences, the medical arts, magic, alchemy, numerology, astrology, and physiognomy. It concluded that a wise and moral ruler is a good ruler who will be supported by the people.

Figure 5 Aristotle teaching Alexander the Great, Royal Manuscripts, British Library

4. From Mysticism to Christianity

When Christianity began to spread, the known world was still steeped in the Mysteries. Once only an oral tradition, since Aristotle and Alexander, some of the wisdom of these Mysteries was being recorded by scribes into texts and scrolls for the priesthood and for the great libraries. As individualism and intellect grew, the mysteries faded. Hastening their decline, many a conqueror had forced hierophants to perform initiations upon them. Desecration had become common. As a symbol of this decline, Herostratus, seeking notoriety, torched the great Temple of Artemis in Ephesus in 356 BC.

Mithraism and the Mysteries of Mithras

Just before Christianity arrived, a new mystery spread within and beyond the Roman Empire. The new mystery, Mithraism, seemed to

Figure 6: Aristotle teaching Alexander the Great, Royal Manuscripts, British Library

account for the changing state of the human soul. Begun before the first century and lasting into the fourth this Persian religion spread across the Mediterranean. Known as the Mysteries of Mithras, its rapid spread is attributed to the Roman Legions who carried it with them far into central Europe, even into western Europe. What they had experienced in Persia, where Oriental wisdom and religions mingled, they spread upon the same ground where Christianity would soon grow. Their worship of Mithras was a worship about the invincible sun forces within each person. In this, the Mithraic religion had feelings that were surprisingly similar to Early Christian sentiments of Christ's role as the Sun God. By arriving before Christianity, the religion knew nothing, of course, of what was to happen on Golgotha. Throughout what was the Roman Empire numerous archaeological sites have been found. These include meeting places, monuments, and artifacts of Mithraism.

At its core were the Mithraic Mysteries. These mysteries claimed Zoroaster as its founder. This has led to speculation that the three Magi who visit the baby Jesus, as described in Matthew's Gospel, were not only Zoroastrian astrologers but, more importantly, Mithraic

Figure 7 Mithras slaying the bull beneath the Invincible Sun God, Vatican Museum

initiates. Does this offer an insight to link these two religions? The historian of Greek religion, Walter Burkert, writes, "Mithraism was not an alternative to other pagan religions, but rather a particular way of practicing pagan worship. Many Mithraic initiates can also be found worshipping in the civic religion and as initiates of other mystery cults."[45] As such, the Mithraic mysteries had no 'public' face. Only their initiates could participate in its worship service and this only in the secrecy of the Mithraeum. In this way, its practice had a similar relationship to pagan religions as Freemasonry does to Christian and other religions.

The main symbol of Mithraism showed the God Mithras riding on a bull. Above him were the starry heavens to which he belonged. Below him the earth to which the bull belonged. This story, like the Greek myths, contained pictures of what the human soul must go through in order to commune again with God. The human had to conquer their inner animal nature depicted as the bull. Something new in the human had to be born that could arise out of the human that had become chained by materialism, like Prometheus, to the mineral kingdom, the rock. Then, once freed from the rock, the human

---

[45] Walter Burkert, *Ancient Mystery Cults*. Harvard University Press, 1987, p. 49

soul then had to conquer its animal nature, its temptations of the flesh, as symbolize by the bull. Finally, the perfected human could commune, could feast, with the God of the Sun. Zoroaster had called this God of the Sun, Ahura Mazdao. Early Christians believed that the Cosmic Christ had descended to inhabit the body of Jesus of Nazareth. Rudolf Steiner describes this in his lectures *From Jesus to Christ*.[46] Father of the Church, Clement of

[46] Rudolf Steiner, *From Jesus to Christ*, 4Oct1911, Carlsruhe, GA 131

Alexandria spoke of Christ driving his chariot across the sky.[47]

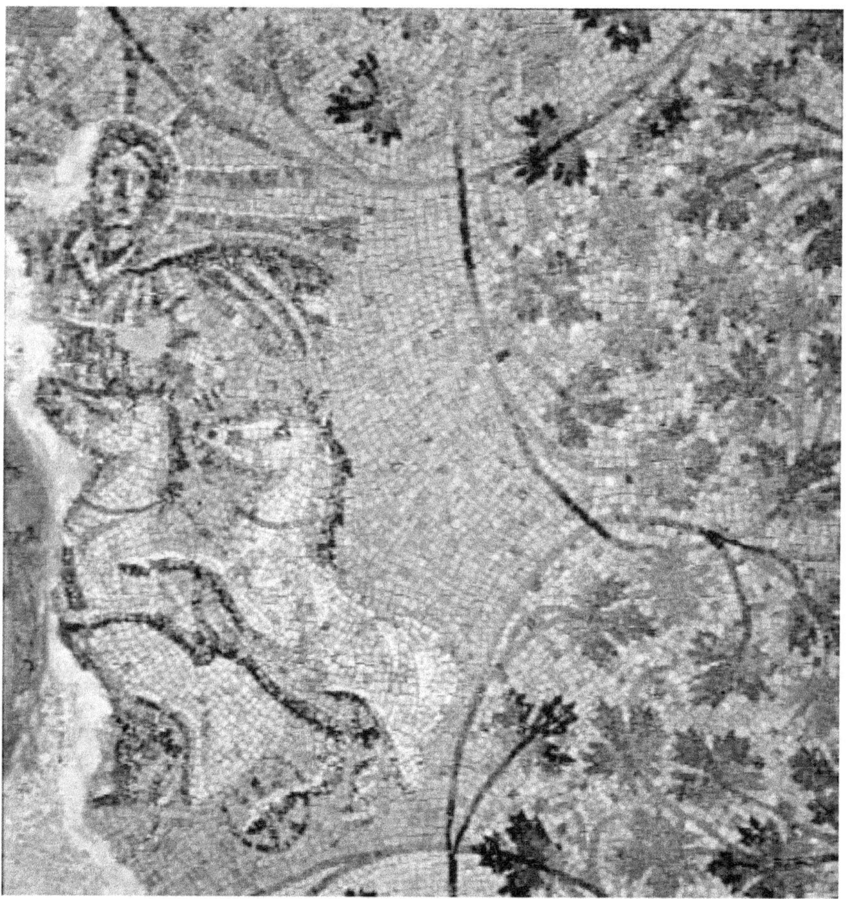

Figure 8 Christ as Invincible Sun, necropolis under St. Peter's mid-third century, Grotte Vaticane, Rome

This mosaic is in an Early Christian tomb.

---

[47] Matilda Webb, *The Churches and Catacombs of Early Christian Rome,* Sussex Academic Press, 2001, p. 18

The Mysteries of Mithras had seven grades of initiation. Initiates called themselves syndexioi, meaning those united by the handshake.[48] Again, note, by the handshake, the similarity to Freemasonry. They built underground temples, called mithraea (singular mithraeum). Many of these temples still exist as archeological sites.

The development of courage was stressed in their mysteries. "Whereas the Greek disciple was affected by a deep feeling of reverence, to the Mithraic disciple alone was given the knowledge of the terrible and awe-inspiring powers in Nature so that he felt himself infinitesimally small in comparison. So powerful was this impression, consequent upon his alienation from the primal source of being, that he felt that in its vastness the Universe could at any moment overwhelm and annihilate him."[49]

"The Greek disciple became fearless through the setting free of his powers. The Mithraic disciple was brought so far that he drank in the greatness of Cosmic Thought, and thereby his

---

[48] Manfred Clauss, *The Roman Cult of Mithras*, Routledge, 2001, p. 42

[49] Rudolf Steiner, *From Jesus to Christ*, 4Oct1911, Carlsruhe, GA 131

soul also became strong and courageous. A knowledge of the dignity and value of a human being was gained, and with it a feeling for truth and fidelity. The disciple learned to recognize that man must always hold himself under control during his earthly existence."[50]

As we shall see, Early Christianity had many streams. In the spread of Eastern Christianity as well as the spread of Arian Christianity in the West, we can find a Mithraic element in it. Its appeal to the inner warrior found in Mithraism is also found in the Gothic tribes when they converted to Arian Christianity. Later we will cover the translation by Ulfilas of the Bible into the Gothic language. When this Bible is further translated into a modern language, it remains imperfect if one is unaware that Mithraic elements, such as fearlessness, that played into the terminology used by the initiate Ulfilas to convert the Gothic tribes.

The Apostolic Age

Throughout the remainder of this chapter, we should keep in mind that what has been recorded about the other forms of Christianity,

---

[50] Rudolf Steiner, *From Jesus to Christ*, 4Oct1911, Carlsruhe, GA 131

such as Arian, was written by those who defeated those "heretical" beliefs. In the middle of the twentieth century, the discovery of the Dead Sea Scrolls and the texts at Nag Hamadi has allowed scholars new insights into these early Christianities. But still, we have only a few fragments of the literary works of the Gnostics, Manicheans, Mithraists, and so many others.

The first decades after the first Christian Pentecost are called the Apostolic Age. The twelve apostles, as united individuals, each took up their calling. They went forth into the world carrying on the oral trainings that they had received. Without books they continued with oral teachings. How did these apostles find the courage take up their calling? They apparently developed an inner fortitude during the fifty days that followed the event on Golgotha when, according to Christian theology, Christ, now resurrected, instructed and prepared the twelve for their change from disciple to apostle. They established communities based on Christian principles. These early communities were largely within larger Jewish communities at first. They proclaimed Christ was a fulfillment of Jewish prophecies. Thus, they remained Jewish in character, continuing its traditions.

The person most credited with establishing Christianity outside of Jewish communities was the Jewish scholar Saul. Because the stories of Christ did not fit with his expectations of a Jewish Messiah, Saul sought to stop this movement of early Christianity. But on his way to Damascus to persecute Christians there, Saul went through his conversion – a 3.5-day initiation. Afterward, like initiates of the Mysteries before him, he changed his name from Saul to Paul. With his added apostleship, the communities expanded into Hellenistic communities where pagan religions associated with the ancient Mysteries had ruled for thousands of years. The expansion out of Judaism proved to be very difficult for some of the apostles, notably Peter.[51] This shows that

---

[51] Richard Valantasis, *The Beliefnet Guide to Gnosticiam and Other Vanished Christianities*, 2006. In the *Gospel of Mary*, Peter unsuccessfully argued that "Jesus would not have revealed such important teachings to a woman," and that "her stature cannot be greater than that of the male apostles." Also, in Galatians 2:12-16, "But afterward, when some friends of James came, Peter wouldn't eat with the Gentiles anymore. He was afraid of criticism from these people who insisted on the necessity of circumcision. As a result, other Jewish believers followed Peter's hypocrisy, and even Barnabas

the 'training' in Christianity, even for the apostles, was an on-going process.

Dionysius, and the Esoteric Christian School of Athens

Paul established the esoteric School of Athens with Dionysius the Areopagite (first century) its principal. It appears to have operated similarly to a mystery school. Dionysius taught that the forces of the sun, astronomical and cosmic, entered into the earth sphere with the Christ. This became possible when he united with the man Jesus of Nazareth. Thereby a totally new relationship came into being between the earth, mankind, and all the higher hierarchies. It was a penetration of this teaching of the hierarchies with the ancient astronomy that could be found in the original

---

was led astray by their hypocrisy. When I [Paul] saw that they were not following the truth of the gospel message, I said to Peter in front of all the others, "Since you, a Jew by birth, have discarded the Jewish laws and are living like a Gentile, why are you now trying to make these Gentiles follow the Jewish traditions? "You and I are Jews by birth, not 'sinners' like the Gentiles. Yet we know that a person is made right with God by faith in Jesus Christ, not by obeying the law. And we have believed in Christ Jesus, so that we might be made right with God because of our faith in Christ, not because we have obeyed the law. For no one will ever be made right with God by obeying the law."

works of Dionysius the Areopagite. As in other esoteric schools, successors to Dionysius took on his name as a title. The school lasted until 529 when an edict by Emperor Justinian closed all such schools.

The Spiritual Hierarchy

Dionysius named nine levels of the heavenly hierarchy and described each as well as their level's role. Closest to humanity, in their model, were the angels, then the archangels, and the archai. Above these three were the Exusiai (or Elohim in Hebrew), Dynamis, and Kyriotetes. The highest three were called the Thrones, the Cherubim, and the Seraphim.

These names show up throughout biblical texts but are often translated to words such as Power, Might, and Dominion [over] when the designation of a spiritual being was not clear to the translator. In Colossians 1:16 we read in Greek, "θρόνοι εἴτε κυριότητες εἴτε ἀρχαὶ εἴτε ἐξουσίαι" whose literal translation is "thronoi or kyriotētes or archai or exousiai" but which is translated (NIV) as "thrones or powers or rulers or authorities." Here we see an example of monism of the biblical author being translated according to the dualism of the translator and his audience. The author, however, wrote with a monistic understanding; that is, there is a spiritual being that is each of these concepts.

When we read in the New Testament, we need to keep in mind that the author had indivisible meaning in mind. For example, we read: "Truly, truly I say to you, unless one is born of water and the spirit, he cannot enter into the kingdom of God ... The wind blows where it wishes and you hear the sound of it, but do not know where it comes from and where it is going; so is everyone who is born of the spirit."[52] The translator decided to use two different words for "spirit" and "wind" although both are the Greek word "pneuma". Some translators will use "breath". Linguist Owen Barfield spoke of this translation problem, "We must, therefore, imagine a time, when 'spiritus' [Latin] or 'pneuma' [Greek] or older words from which these had descended, meant neither breath, nor wind, nor spirit, nor yet all three of these things, but when they simply had their own old peculiar meaning, which has since, in the course of the evolution

---

[52] John 3:5-8

of consciousness, crystallized into the three meanings specified."[53]

Rudolf Steiner describes how the original works of Dionysius were obfuscated, "In the sixth century, the attempt was made to obliterate the traces even of the more ancient teachings by Dionysius the Areopagite. They were altered in such a way that they now represented merely an abstract teaching of the spirit. In the form in which the teaching of Dionysius the Areopagite has come down to us, it is a spiritual teaching that no longer has much to do with etheric astronomy. This is the reason he is then called the 'Pseudo-Dionysius.' In this manner, the decline of the teaching of wisdom was brought about. On the one hand, the teachings of Dionysius were distorted; on the other hand, the truly alive teaching in Athens that had tried to unite etheric astronomy with Christianity was eradicated. Finally, in regard to the cultic aspect, the Mithras worship was exterminated."[54]

---

[53] Owen Barfield, *Poetic Diction: A Study in Meaning*. Middletown CT: Wesleyan University Press. Originally published in 1928. 2nd ed. 1973, pp. 79-81

[54] Rudolf Steiner, *Materialism and the Task of Anthroposophy*, lecture 4, 15Apr1921, Dornach, GA 204

Mysticism in the First Three Centuries

According to University of Chicago's Divinity School professor, Bernard McGinn, Christian Mystics held that, "the core of mysticism [was] understood as inner transformation" and the "encounter with God transforms their minds and their lives."[55] McGinn adds that the Christian mystic "wants to penetrate to the living source of the biblical message, that is, to the Divine Word."[56] Leonardo da Vinci similarly wrote, "for he who has access to the fountain does not go to the water-jar."[57] The Gospels were deemed to have been written by Christian mystics and, as such, its words have meaning on multiple levels. "Mystical interpretation was not arbitrary, but was governed by two essential criteria: first, the usefulness of the reading for encouraging deeper contact with God; and second, the reading's coherence with the faith [and knowledge] of the community."[58] McGinn

---

[55] Bernard McGinn, *The Essential Writings of Christian Mysticism*, Random House, 2006

[56] IBID

[57] The Notebooks of Leonardo Da Vinci, Chapter 9, translated by Jean Paul Richter

[58] IBID

describes the mysticism of some fifty different Christian mystics.

Iamblichus

Not all mystics were Christian of course. Iamblichus (245 – 325) exemplifies the non-Christian mystic thinkers during the transition period from the Apostolic Age to the Decrees of Theodosius I (381 – 391) when Orthodox Christianity became the only tolerated religion of the Roman Empire. Mysticism in this time period mingled with intellectualism and, of course, philosophy. Iamblichus based his non-Christian mysticism[59] on the trinity who he saw as composed of:

1. The Monad: a transcendent incommunicable "One"
2. The Dyad: a second super-existent "One" who, like Christ, stands between the Monad and 'the many' and produced the intellect, or soul, psyche.
3. The Triad: the realized intellect in which true thinking exists and is similar

---

[59] C. Whittingham, *Iamblichus on the Mysteries of the Egyptians, Chaldeans, and Assyrians*, 1821. See online book copy: https://books.google.com/books?id=wb8vAAAAYAAJ&source=gbs_navlinks_s.

to the Christian concept of the Holy Spirit.

We will see how concepts such as these played into the Christian battles concerning the Trinity. Iamblichus, a pre-Muslim Arab, studied Neoplatonism under Porphyry who was a pupil of its founder, Plotinus. Iamblichus, imbued with the materialism of his time, believed that just like the soul, matter was as divinely created. Because of matter's divine source, the soul could embody [incarnate] into it. We experience the change in philosophy, even within the same stream, brought about by materialism when we find that Plotinus had reasoned that the soul would not and could not operate from within a physical body. Rather, it operated the body like an avatar. With Iamblichus, the emerging materialism and the loss of the ancient mysteries was cause for a change in philosophy.

Near the Christian community of Antioch in 304 in a Syrian city that was famous for its Neoplatonic philosophers, Iamblichus established his own school where he taught Platonic conceptions. His intention was to reassert a mystical and mythical interpretation into Hellenistic and Neoplatonic philosophy.[60] His expertise was more than Greek ancient Mysteries but also the Egyptian Mysteries as evident in a book attributed to him, *De Mysteriis Aegyptiorum*. And the mystic he held in highest esteem was Egyptian-educated Pythagoras and his metempsychosis or the "transmigration of souls," i.e. reincarnation. He holds in the highest regard Pythagoras as evident in his multiple books that weave together mathematics, philosophy, and theology in a Pythagorean way.[61]

Christian Mysticism

Secret Teachings

Around each apostle were the next generation of disciples who listened and absorbed all that they could. The writers of the three so-called synoptic gospels came from this second generation. Within these circles were teachings and rituals that remained secret. In this regard, early esoteric Christianity practiced similarly to the ancient Mysteries. This included the prohibition against the wrongful

---

[60] Gregory Shaw, 'Neoplatonism I: Antiquity', *Dictionary of Gnosis & Western Esotericism*, ed. by Wouter J. Hanegraff, Leiden & Boston: Brill, 2006

[61] Thomas Taylor ed, *The Life of Pythagoras by Iamblichus*, Krotona, 1918

divulging of knowledge. Secret trainings are mentioned throughout the writings of this second generation. Here are two examples from the Nag Hammadi collection of Gnostic texts that date from the first decades after Ascension:

1. Of several mystical passages, the *Gospel of Thomas* contains these two passages, (1) “These are the hidden [or occult] words that the living Jesus spoke and Didymus Judas Thomas wrote them down” and (2) “Now when Thomas came to his companions (the other disciples), they asked him: ‘What did Jesus say unto thee?’ Thomas said to them: ‘If I tell you one of the words which he said to me, you will take up stones and throw them at me; and a fire will come out of the stones and devour you.”[62] Divulging the secrets of the ancient Mysteries was viewed as a betrayal punishable by death. Hearing such secrets by one unprepared was deemed to be extremely dangerous to

---

[62] *The Gospel of Thomas*, translated by Stephen Patterson and Marvin Meyer, http://gnosis.org/naghamm/gosthom.html accessed 21June2018

their well-being. [Note: Didymus (Greek) and Thomas (Aramaic) both mean "twin"].

2. The *Secret Book of James* begins with, "You have asked me to send you a secret book revealed to Peter and me by the master, and I could not turn you down, nor could I speak to you, so I have written it in Hebrew and have sent it to you, and to you alone. But since you are a minister of the salvation of the saints, try to be careful not to reveal to many people this book that the savior did not want to reveal even to all of us, his twelve students. ... Ten months ago, I sent you another secret book that the savior revealed to me."[63]

Recall that until these texts from the Nag Hammadi collection only became known after 1945. All that was known by scholars of Christian Gnosticism (and other so-called heresies) before 1945 was from books written by those who had exterminated them. Their books were written to justify their 'un-Christian' slaughter and the destruction of the

[63] *The Secret Book of James* from Nag Hammadi collection

Gnostic (and other heretical) texts, schools, and relics. Obviously, these accounts and their analysis done by the heresy hunting victors cannot be trusted.

Secret Mark and Esoteric Christianity

The Christian Gnostic texts found at Nag Hammadi were not the only early texts with esoteric underpinnings. The Gospel writer Mark also wrote about hidden Christian knowledge and initiations. *Secret Mark* is one. Early Christianity historians, J.D. Crossan and Helmut Koester, reason that St. Mark first wrote his *Secret Mark* and later wrote the *Gospel of Mark* by removing its esoteric passages. Helmut Koester writes: "It is immediately evident that this story shows many similarities with the story of the raising of Lazarus in John 11." A book's authenticity required the author to be an initiate or a reliable witness to an apostle. Koester indicates both are inherent in *Secret Mark*.[64]

Secret Mark was discovered by Columbia University professor Morton Smith in 1958. It is a handwritten copy of a letter by Church Father Clement of Alexandria (c. 150 – c. 215).

---

[64] Helmut Koester, *Ancient Christian Gospels*, Trinity Press International, 1990

The copy had been placed in the back of a book that had been printed in the eighteenth century. The book itself was an interesting compilation of works by Church Father Ignatius of Antioch. Smith found this book in the library of the ancient monastery of Mar Saba that is situated just south-east of Jerusalem. Morton Smith announced his find in 1960 and then published the letter along with his interpretation in 1973.[65]

Later that year, the library of the Greek Orthodox Church in Jerusalem accepted the actual letter for its archive. Yet sometime after 1990, the letter was, inexplicably, lost. Luckily, Morton Smith had photographed it. Controversy about its authenticity then raged for two decades. Today, nearly all scholars, persuaded mostly by Scott G. Brown's research,[66] now accept its authenticity. But the stain on it as a hoax remains in the public unfortunately.

---

[65] http://www.earlychristianwritings.com/secretmark.html

[66] Scott G. Brown, *Mark's Other Gospel: Rethinking Morton Smith's Controversial Discovery, Studies in Christianity and Judaism*, Waterloo, Ont., Canada: Wilfrid Laurier University Press, 2005

After a greeting, the letter states, "As for Mark, then, during Peter`s stay in Rome he wrote an account of the Lord`s doings, not, however, declaring all of them, nor yet hinting at the secret ones, but selecting what he thought most useful for increasing the faith of those who were being instructed."[67] Note that within this group, individuals were receiving secret knowledge and a training that led to the new Christian initiation.

Secret Mark continues, "As for Mark, then, during Peter's stay in Rome he wrote an account of the Lord's doings, not, however, declaring all of them, nor yet hinting at the secret ones, but selecting what he thought most useful for increasing the faith of those who were being instructed. But when Peter died a martyr, Mark came over to Alexandria, bringing both his own notes and those of Peter, from which he transferred to his former book the things suitable to whatever makes for progress toward knowledge.

"Thus, he composed a more spiritual Gospel for the use of those who were being *perfected* [my emphasis]. Nevertheless, he yet did not

---

[67] http://gnosis.org/library/secm.htm

divulge the things not to be uttered, nor did he write down the hierophantic teaching of the Lord, but to the stories already written he added yet others and, moreover, brought in certain sayings of which he knew the interpretation would, as a mystagogue, lead the hearers into the innermost sanctuary of that Truth hidden by seven veils.

"Thus, in sum, he prepared matters, neither grudgingly nor incautiously, in my opinion, and, dying, he left his composition to the church in Alexandria, where it even yet is most carefully guarded, being read only to those who are being initiated into the great mysteries." –Clement of Alexandria. Note the words "whatever makes for progress toward knowledge!" This was clearly a path of Knowledge at this time and it was akin to Christian Gnosticism.

The Weaving of Knowledge and Mysticism: Rosicrucianism

This path of Knowledge would vanish only to reappear at the start of the Renaissance. Similar to these heretics of Early Christianity, Leonardo da Vinci and others sought knowledge as a path to the divine. The Platonic Academy of Florence was modeled after the esoteric Christian School of Athens run by Dionysius the Areopagite with the same name, the Platonic Academy. Founding this Florentine school was inspired by the lectures of Gemistus Plethon. It was established by Cosimo de Medici and led by Marsilio Facino.

Leonardo would learn much within these walls and within the Garden of San Marcos and its library. The thirst for Knowledge was partially quenched by texts that came to Italy from the East. We do not know where the trunk load of texts brought by Plethon in 1438 ended up, but likely this served as the fountain of knowledge seekers like Leonardo. With wisdom gained from this fountain, Leonardo could see through the dogmas that had become established and how the Church stood as the biggest obstacle to the Knowledge that wished to be realized in the era of the Renaissance.

Before the Renaissance, mysticism had come to Florence and other parts of Europe through the Cathars and through the Knights Templar. Kabbalists fleeing Spain arrived in Florence and nearby towns bringing Jewish mysticism. Like mystic groups before them, what transpired within initiation ceremonies remained secret.

Little of its wisdom was understood but its fruits were cherished.

Mysticism has managed to persist with its few gems of revealed wisdom throughout the centuries. Traditions were maintained by Freemasonry and other such societies. A new mystical practice arose with Rosicrucianism starting in the fourteenth century but not well known until the seventeenth century when three books were published anonymously. These have been attributed to Johann Valentin Andreae (1568–1654), a Lutheran theologian.[68] A member would never reveal their membership, but many great writers have been surmised to have been Rosicrucians. Lord Byron, in his story, *Cain a Mystery* (1821), claimed he had written in accordance with the old "very profane" mysteries. In these ancient mysteries cited by Byron, Lucifer reigned

---

[68] The three books were *Fama Fraternitatis of the Meritorious Order of the Rosy Cross* (1614), *The Confession of the Rosicrucian Fraternity* (1615), and *The Chymical Marriage of Christian Rosenkreuz* (1616). These recount the travels of Christian Rosenkreuz, the founder of the group, who was born in 1378 and supposedly lived for 106 years.

together with Jehovah, “Lucifer: No, we reign together; but our dwellings are asunder.”[69]

Gnosticism

This Christian sect took its name from the Greek term *gnostikos* which means "having knowledge." These Gnostics believed in a Fall of Mankind from being in the bosom of the omniscient One, God. Because of our origin with God, we carry a divine spark, a spiritual light. Despite now being in a world of darkness, of matter, through a path of knowledge, one can develop this inner light to eventually come to the experience of God. They found in John 1:4 “In Him is life. And life is the light of Men” the confirmation for this belief.

They were certain that coming to an experience of God had been possible for initiates of the Mysteries. Moreover, it was through a Cosmic Christ who was experienced as one of the heavenly hosts (e.g., archangel or angel) that these initiates were guided to this ecstatic experience. They believed that this Cosmic Christ had been born into Jesus of Nazareth so that all people could become

---

[69] Lord Byron, *Cain a Mystery*, Carlile, 1822, https://books.google.com/books?id=HeAtAAAAYAAJ

reunited with the all-knowing One through a path of knowledge.

The Gnostics looked to Plato and Aristotle as sources for their knowledge-based path to perfection of the soul. Plato had claimed that a certain god, the Demiurge, had created the physical world for mankind following the Fall. This Demiurge figured into several of the Christian sects of the second century including the Gnostics.

"Matter is evil!" supposedly was the crux of Gnostic theology. Borrowed from certain Greek philosophers, this idea stood its ground against the emerging Catholic teaching. Opposition to Gnosticism pointed to Genesis 1:31 "And God saw everything that he had made, and behold, it was very good" as evidence that matter could not be part of evil. Because of its negative view of matter, Gnosticism had difficulty with the concept of a full Incarnation of soul and spirit into the physical, especially for a divine being. They reasoned, if matter is evil, then every human would be unsuitable for the incarnation of a God. With a body of matter, Jesus could not be the true God. And since Christ, a divine being, is in no way evil, he could not have been a true man. Thus, many Gnostics denied the Incarnation, claiming that Christ only directed Jesus like an avatar. Thus, Christ's humanity was merely an illusion.

Some Gnostics went so far as claiming that the God of the Jews must be an evil deity because their texts, the Old Testament, taught that God created matter. The God of Jesus Christ, as described in the New Testament must be a different God. This question of the Jewish God and the Christian Father God being the same God rises up often during the first few centuries. The Gnostics also proposed belief in a hierarchy of divine beings. Jesus was the man whom Christ took control of at the baptism and then left on the cross. They pointed to Matthew 27:46, "My God, my God, why have you forsaken me?" as proof.

They divided the divine realm into twelve "aeons". This led to the development of a science of these spiritual realms. Gnostic ideas were, however, expressed spatially. Interestingly, the role of time as an idea was unimportant to their cosmology. Perhaps, in that era, Gnostic understanding was not yet capable of understanding time completely. The theological evolution from the Gnostics to

Clement of Alexandria brought the concept of time into the evolution of the Christ. Clement taught that the Christ had existed in prior ages revealing himself through angels before he did as the Son.

The writings of Paul and John both have Gnostic concepts and symbols employed. Debate continues among scholars as to who influenced whom; did the Gnostics borrow from John and Paul or were these authors writing under a Gnostic influence?

These Gnostics apparently offered praise to spirits such as Lucifer and individuals such as Cain.[70] In his book *Against Heresies* written in 180 CE, Irenaeus attacked the Gnostic Christians whom he calls Cainites. Irenaeus wanted to keep such biblical villains in hell. The Gnostics did not condone these sins but knew that Christ's deeds had redeemed them. This encompassing fullness of Gnostic spiritual wisdom was mostly lost by the third century, as materialism and heresy hunting had weeded it out of human understanding.

---

[70] C. B. Smith II, *No Longer Jews: The Search for Gnostic Origins*, Hendrickson, 2004

The Gospel of Judas

Thus, the story of Judas deserves special mention here for Judas Iscariot was Christ's contemporary. Christian theology has declared for centuries that Judas betrayed Christ and thereby caused his death. One Gnostic text condemned by the heresy hunter Irenaeus was the *Gospel of Judas.* Historians knew it once existed by references, but they could not find this text until viewed in 1983[71] when it was discovered within a codex. Originally containing 31 pages with writing on both sides, when it came to market in 1999, only 13 pages survived. Carbon 14 has dated this codex to between 220 and 320. The gospel was written in Greek sometime before 180, during the time of the collisions of multiple Christianities, and was translated to the Egyptian Coptic script found in this codex.

The Gnostic *Gospel of Judas* offers a dramatically different view of Judas than that held for nearly two thousand years of Christian condemnation of Judas as the betrayer of

---

[71] Stephen Emmel, professor of Coptic studies at the Univ. of Munster, realized what this document was that had been discovered with other texts in 1970s near Beni Masar, Egypt. An English translation was published in 2006 by the National Geographic Society.

Christ-Jesus. When the four Gospels of the New Testament speak of Judas, they use the word "paradidómi" which is often translated as "betray." But several scholars have pointed out that this word, according to Strong's Concordance, actually means "to hand over, to give or deliver over." Such a translation would be more fitting to the theme of the *Gospel of Judas* than the word "betrays" for this Gnostic text portrays Judas as performing Christ-Jesus' request! Of course, not all professors of Biblical studies agree that this Gnostic gospel should be considered part of the canon. For example, April DeConick, holds to the traditional view Judas as the betrayer.[72]

A team of scholars was assembled in 2005 to examine and study this codex. Rodolphe Kasser, regarded as one of the world's preeminent Coptic scholars, headed the team that included Bart Ehrman, Stephen Emmel, Gregor Wurst, Craig Evans, Marvin Meyer, Elaine Pagels, and Donald Senior. Kasser remarked that "this lost gospel, providing information on Judas Iscariot—considered for 20 centuries and by hundreds of millions of

---

[72] April DeConick, The Thirteenth Apostle: What the Gospel of Judas Really Says, Continuum, 2nd Ed., 2009

believers as an antichrist of the worst kind—bears witness to something completely different from what was said [about Judas] in the Bible." Elaine Pagels concluded that Judas is portrayed as having a mission to hand Jesus over to the soldiers claiming that Bible translators have mistranslated the Greek word for "handing over" to "betrayal".[73]

The May 2006 issue of National Geographic magazine was devoted to highlighting this work. Stephen Emmel, a Coptic studies professor at the University of Münster in Germany added, "I expect this gospel to be important mainly for the deeper insight it will give scholars into the thoughts and beliefs of certain Christians in the second century of the Christian era, namely the Gnostics." Not only did this text offer an alternative view of the relationship between Jesus and Judas. It illustrated the diversity of early Christian theology.

The New Testament Gospels seem to claim that Judas betrayed Jesus for "30 pieces of silver." He then had to identify Christ for the Roman soldiers and did so with a kiss. Later,

---

[73] Elaine Pagels, *Reading Judas: The Gospel of Judas and the Shaping of Christianity*, Penguin, 2007

Judas returns the bribe and commits suicide, according to the four gospels.

The *Gospel of Judas* offered a different insight

into Judas' motivation. The text begins by announcing that it is the "*secret account* of the

Figure 9 "The Kiss of Judas" Giotto c. 1306, Scrovegni Chapel, Padua

revelation that Jesus over three days spoke to Judas Iscariot during the week before Passover." This gospel described Judas as

Jesus' closest friend and the one who could truly understand His mission. Thus, Judas was selected for a special role among Jesus' disciples, to hand Him over for eventual execution. In these conversations, Christ revealed that He was to be the necessary sacrifice, that His death would change the course of Earthly and Human evolution. Christ said to Judas, "you will exceed all of them, for you will sacrifice the man that clothes me." Here Christ told Judas that his physical body is like clothing; it will be shed at death as the Sacrifice.

Of these words, Kasser felt "[Christ-]Jesus said it was necessary for someone to free him finally from his human body, and he preferred that this liberation be done by a friend rather than by an enemy." [74]

Bart Ehrman, chair of the Department of Religious Studies at the University of North Carolina at Chapel Hill concluded that "this gospel has a completely different understanding of God, the world, Christ, salvation, human existence—not to mention of

---

74 https://www.nationalgeographic.com/science/2006/04/lost-gospel-judas-revealed-jesus-archaeology/

Judas himself—than came to be embodied in the Christian creeds and canon."[75]

Reverend Donald Senior, president of the Catholic Theological Union in Chicago, Illinois points out that "this ancient text helps the modern world rediscover something that the early Christians knew firsthand. In the early centuries of the Christian era there were multiple sacred texts resulting from communities in various parts of the Mediterranean world trying to come to grips with the meaning of Jesus Christ for their lives."[76]

In this gospel, it is Judas Iscariot who is singled out as Jesus' greatest disciple. He alone is able to receive Jesus' most profound teaching and revelation. Judas is able to stand before Jesus. "I know who you are and from where you have come. You are from the immortal realm of Barbelo.[77] And I am not worthy to utter the

---

[75] IBID

[76] IBID

[77] According to Irenaeus, chapter 29 of *Against Heresies*, Barbelo means "The virgin spirit [who] has a never-changing Aeon" -- see http://www.unifr.ch/bkv/kapitel609.htm. There are twelve aeons in Gnostic traditions.

name of the one who has sent you."[78] After this confession Jesus teaches Judas in private.

At the conclusion of this private teaching, Jesus offers these words about his death as a sacrifice for all: "You will exceed them all. For you will sacrifice the man who clothes me."[79] Judas will carry out the sacrifice that truly counts, the sacrifice that will result in salvation. He will sacrifice the physical body of Jesus, thus allowing Christ-Jesus to complete his mission.

Gnostic History

Gnosticism is a term first used by the English philosopher of religion Henry More (1614–87). He used it to refer to the multiple religious groups who sought union with God through knowledge. He derived it from ancient sources that referred to such a group as gnostikoi (Greek: "those who have gnosis i.e., knowledge"). Such religious and philosophical movements flourished during Greco-Roman times when, after Alexander, the oral wisdom

---

[78] Rodolphe Kasser, Marvin Meyer, and Gregor Wurst, *The Gospel of Judas*, The National Geographic Society, 2006, page 35, lines 15-21
[79] IBID, page 56, lines 18-20

of the ancient mystery centers flowed into the various libraries.

Gnosticism, which began before the time of Christ, was at its peak in the second century when the multiple Christianities were in their infancy. The merging of these two naturally took place. Gnostics were the "assimilationists of those early centuries of Christianity itself."[80] From the perspective of a Gnostic initiate, there was truth in the Greek and Egyptian mysteries as well as in Christianity. German scholar, Kurt Rudolph, in his book *The Nature and History of Gnosticism*, adds "the Christianizing of Gnosis and the Gnosticizing of Christianity. The result of both processes is the canonization of Christianity as an Orthodox Church on the one hand, and the elimination of Gnosis as a heresy on the other."[81]

Thus, the foundations for what became known as Gnosticism had been established some three hundred years before Christianity as an outgrowth of Alexandrianism. When Early Christianity arrived, one of the Christianities,

---

[80] Nicola Denzey Lewis, *Introduction to Gnosticism: Ancient Voices, Christian Worlds*, Oxford University Press, 2012

[81] Kurt Rudolph, *The Nature and History of Gnosticism*, HarperOne, 1987

probably originating in Alexandria, grew out of the already existing Gnosticism. Christian Gnosticism flourished for a couple centuries before the emerging proto-Orthodox Christianity struggled to separate itself from Gnostic dualistic[82] philosophies. During the two hundred years it took from Irenaeus (130 – 202) to the decrees of Theodosius I (381 – 391), the theological debates, sometimes deadly, raged on. Christianity struggled with concepts about the Trinity: about who beget whom, about the substance for each divinity, and about who created what.

There were (violent) debates about the Father God. Some, such as Marcion (85 – 160), said that the God in the Old Testament whose moral creed was "Your eyes must not show pity—life for life, eye for eye, tooth for tooth"[83] could not be the same God of love and mercy to whom Christ prayed as his Father. Even the question of what was God-the-Father's name was debated? Since it had

---

[82] Dualism sees heaven (or spirit) and earth (or matter) as separate, even separate creations. Monism sees just one as real. Spiritual monism sees the spirit as real and matter as illusion while materialistic monism sees only matter as real and all spiritual concepts as illusion.
[83] Deuteronomy 19:21

been ineffable, could it be translated as Jehovah or Yahweh? Were either of these the Father God to whom Christ prayed? Could Yahweh have been (just) one member of the Elohim (aka Exusiai)? (The word "Elohim" is plural. Some groups claim there were seven Elohim comprising the "Pleroma" mentioned in Genesis and often translated as "fullness".)

The chart below includes several Christian Gnostic groups that were condemned and subsequently destroyed. In most cases, texts and relics of the various Gnostic groups were burned so that what we know of them comes from those who condemned them.

More Gnostic groups will be discussed later in this chapter.

Heresy	Theology	History	Who Condemned	Comment
Naassenes	Trace their doctrines to Mariamne, a disciple of James, brother of Jesus	Active by 100	Hippolytus of Rome ~250	Book V of *Ref. of All Heresies*
Ophites and Sethians	Lucifer gave Freedom to Adam & Eve, thus a hero. OT God is enemy of worldly knowledge	Active by 100	Hippolytus of Rome ~250	Belief based on *Apocalypse of Adam*
Manichaeism	Man is mixture of good & evil, spiritual world & physical = 2 creations	Founded by Mani, 210–276	Theodosius I, decrees 382-391	Huge movement east of Roman empire till 1600s
Valentianism	Christian Gnosticism	Bishop Valentinus, 100-160	Irenaeus and Epiphanius of Salamis, 180	
Paulicians	Christian Gnosticism	Constantine of Mananalis d 684	Empress Theodora II in 843	Spread from Armenia
Priscillianism	Gnostic and Manichaean	Priscillian, 4th C from doctrines by Marcus	Synod of Zaragoza in 380 and Synod of Braga 561	Death decrees brought it to an end in 6th C

As we shall see, Gnosticism found a father in Plato. Like Plato, they found mathematics important for spiritual growth. They said, “Gnosis is Mathesis.” They did not mean by this that the essence of the world can be based on mathematical ideas, but that the first stages in one’s spiritual education are derived from mathematical thought because this could be free of sensory perception. From pondering a mathematical figure, one can learn to know super-sensible facts as they apply to the sense-world. This was fundamental for Plato. One can be trained to visualize the Platonic Idea in a purely spiritual manner if one has worked with mathematical knowledge. Thus, Plato told his students, "learn to emancipate thyself from the senses by mathematics, then mayest thou hope to rise to the comprehension of ideas independently of the senses."

Gnosticism sought something similar. When one reached the stage of being able to think of properties that were independent of sense-perception, then that one was well on their path to spiritual knowledge. Thinking about geometrical forms and arithmetical relations of numbers provided this training. The goal was not to be a mathematician, but to use it as a training for super-sensible knowledge. Geometrical proportions found in the physical world are simple enough for a common point of departure into the spiritual world.

The training in elementary mathematical truths led to an emancipation from a reliance on the senses for knowledge. The Gnostic teacher might have said, "learn to think of the essence of Nature and of Spiritual Being as independently of sense-perception as the mathematician thinks of the circle and its laws, then you may become a student of Gnosticism. You will never find a true Circle in the World. But each circle will confirm in the realm of sense what you have learned about the Circle by super-sensible mathematical perception. Once learned, no experience will ever contradict your super-sensible perception. Thus, you will gain for yourself an imperishable and eternal knowledge."[84]

Mysticism of the Christian Gnostics

Throughout the Gnostic texts of Nag Hammadi there exists the concept of a *perfect*. It refers to a person who, through knowledge, has purified his or her soul to the point that he or she became able to attain clear knowledge of both God and him or herself. Origen wrote in *Principiis* similarly, "For he [Solomon] knew that there were within us two kinds of senses: the one mortal, corruptible, human; the other immortal and intellectual, which he now termed divine. By this divine sense, therefore,

[84] Rudolf Steiner, *Mathematics and Occultism*, lecture, 21Jun1904, GA 35

not of the eyes, but of a pure heart, which is the mind, God may be seen by those who are worthy."[85] Here we find a reference to the one human soul having two aspects: one mortal and directed towards the earth, and the other immortal and directed toward the divine. This becomes an important issue in the Eighth Ecumenical Council.

One who was preparing for his or her first initiation was called a neophyte. The one who conducted the initiation process was called the hierophant. The mystai were those who were already initiated. Typically, there were multiple levels of initiation to successfully pass through before the divine state of God could be experienced. Such steps aligned with the steps that were present in the ancient Mysteries. While it is not known how many initiatory steps existed in the various branches of Gnosticism, likely it was close to the seven steps of initiation found within the Mithraic religion that had spread rapidly through the Roman empire just prior to the arrival of Christianity. These seven stages were likely

[85] Origen, *De Principiis*, Book 1, Chapter 1:9

based on similar stages from the ancient Mysteries. They were:

1. **A Raven** who showed the ability to see life clearly and in its true perspective, could mediate between the external world and the ancestors, thus a messenger.
2. **An Occult One** who was able to receive clairvoyantly the communications from the ancestors as well as the impulses from the gods of the super-sensible world.
3. **A Warrior** who championed the cause of the super-sensible showing he was fit to establish smaller groups within the framework of a larger community.
4. **A Lion** who could establish a union of people with an archangelic being.
5. A Persian (or Israelite or one with one's Folk Soul) who could communicate with a folk-spirit and thus lead an ethnic community in which the ancestors also participated.
6. **A Sun Hero or Sun Runner** who attained to those insights which the Sun Mystery implanted in the human soul. Now union with God could occur.

7. **A Father** who attained the seventh degree of initiation that enabled one to lead humanity towards the fulfillment of God's will in the course of evolution.

We see from this, that one, as a learned individual, could only get to the first level. Each step beyond required greater abilities to work with higher beings and the dead. A hierarchy of spiritual beings was, of course, aligned with this and perceived with each advancement.

Mithraism can be seen as a transition from the enclosed ancient Mysteries to an outflowing esoteric movement open to anyone with the will to perfect his or her own soul. Mithras represented what each human can become when we, like Prometheus, are released from the "rocks" and then can overcome the bull within our nature. The result was to commune with the Sun god, Sol. Like other religions, Mithraism derived from a vision of the coming of Christianity. Like Prometheus, it taught that one must overcome their chains that bind us to the mineral kingdom. Then one must overcome in their inner life that which is impulsive, instinctual like an animal. Finally, the Mithraic initiate could share in a future with the Cosmic Christ who, in religions prior to Christianity, was found as the spiritual being of the sun.

But the Early Christian initiates realized that this Sun Being, this Cosmic Christ, could no longer be found in a higher sphere of consciousness as Mithraism promised. They experienced that the Cosmic Christ had descended to the Earth to be born into the body of Jesus of Nazareth.

Although the practice of initiation vanished by the fourth century, Christian mysticism has persisted throughout Christian history. Many were burned as heretics. Most centuries since the fourth have seen more than a dozen well known Christian mystics. Partial lists with brief biographies can be found online.[86]

Early Christian Initiation and Esotericism

Saul of Tarsus was on his way to persecute members of the new Jewish sect (who would later be called Christians) when he had his spiritual awakening. Details of this event are described in the New Testament book *The Acts of the Apostles*. The text indicates an initiation took place. The signs of this were Saul's

---

[86] See https://en.wikipedia.org/wiki/List_of_Christian_mystics

blindness for 3.5 days, a person who acted as hierophant to bring an end to the blindness, followed by some remarkable change in the individual that led to a name change, i.e., to Paul. All of these are aspects of the initiations once conducted in the ancient Mysteries. From this moment until his death, Paul worked tirelessly as an initiate to bring Christianity to his world, namely the Greek and Latin worlds. Because of his post-Ascension initiation, he brought something more to Christianity than what even the Apostles had been teaching.

We know little to nothing of the steps of the Christian Initiation spoken of in some books and letters such as *Secret Mark*. The scroll, the *Dialogue of the Savior*, contains mystical sequences of seeking, finding, wondering, reigning, and resting as taught by Christ in the *Gospel of Thomas* as well as in the *Gospel of the Hebrews*. The experience on this initiation path of three disciples, namely Thomas, Matthew, and Mariam, was described. These disciples must face fear and the threat of being swallowed up before achieving spirit vision. Part of their experience is full immersion in water. Spirit vision immediately awakened when the disciple emerged from the water.[87]

One might presume that the seven (or fourteen) stations of the cross[88] are related to an early Christian practice of initiation, of perfection. According to Rudolf Steiner, the seven stages of early Christian initiation were:

1. The **Washing of the Feet**, out of humility one honors all 'below' of what you may attain.
2. The **Scourging**, to accept with equanimity the sufferings of life.
3. The **Crowning with Thorns**, to face with courage the exposure of one's defects, our sins.
4. The **Bearing of One's Cross**, Conscience (and karma) active at a worldly scale arises. One strives for virtue. We come to realize that we are much more than

---

[87] Andrew Welburn, The Beginnings of Christianity, Floris Books, 1991, pg. 93

[88] The seven stations were expanded to fourteen. St. Jerome (342-420), while living in Bethlehem, saw crowds of pilgrims from various countries who followed the Way of the Cross. An English pilgrim, William Wey, listed 14 stations in 1462. St. Francis of Assisi wrote a devotional guide for the Stations of the Cross

our physical body, that our body is but the vehicle of our spirit.

5. The **Mystic Death**, at this stage we need to lose all in order to regain all. By losing our own existence, in that moment we appear to die to ourselves, it is in the world around us that we can then begin to live again.
6. The **Entombment**, now freed from one's own body, oneness with the Earth results.
7. The **Resurrection**, this last stage of the Christian initiation transcends all words. At this stage one acquires the power to bring about both healing and disease.[89]

One can see similarities of these seven stages to the seven of the Mithraic initiation.

Roots of Christian Mysticism in the Eleusian Mysteries

One Mystery Center whose practices were partially revealed were the Greek Eleusian Mysteries. Using Marvin Meyer's research,[90]

---

[89] This Early Christian Initiation is described in lecture 8 of Rudolf Steiner's lecture cycle entitled *An Esoteric Cosmology*, 1June1906, Paris, GA 94.

[90] Marvin W. Meyer, *The Ancient Mysteries, a Sourcebook: Sacred Texts of the Mystery Religions of the*

Wikipedia describes their initiation this way. “Inside the Telesterion (the Grand Hall of Initiation), on the 20th Boedromion[91], initiates entered a great hall called Telesterion; in the center stood the Anaktoron ("palace"), which only the hierophants could enter, where sacred objects were stored. Before mystai [those being initiated] could enter the Telesterion, they would recite, "I have fasted, I have drunk the kykeon, I have taken from the kiste ("box") and after working it have put it back in the calathus ("open basket"). ... Combined, these three elements were known as the aporrheta ("unrepeatables"); the penalty for divulging them was death. ... The ban on divulging the core ritual of the Mysteries was thus absolute, which is probably why we know almost nothing about what transpired there. ... [outside several symbolic events take place each day]. On the 23rd of Boedromion, the Mysteries ended, and everyone returned home.”

It was the practice of the mysteries that when someone completed their initiation, that they

---

Ancient Mediterranean World, University of Pennsylvania Press, 1999

[91] Boedromion is a month from the Athenian calendar that corresponds to September/October.

took on a new name because they were no longer their old self. We discussed this when Saul was initiated on his way to Damascus and then took on the name Paul. A remnant of this exists when a cardinal is elected to become the new pope.

Several theologians have come to the conclusion that the Evangelist John (writer of both *John's Gospel* and *Revelations*), was Lazarus. His death experience was his initiation done for the first time in public. After initiation, as was the practice, Lazarus took on a new name, John in honor of the one who had been his guide in the spiritual world before being raised from the dead.[92] Prior to Lazarus, Jewish initiations would be done in the Holy of the Holies. A curtain kept its contents and happenings secret. According to Rudolf Steiner,[93] these initiations consisted of a neophyte being put into a death like state by the hierophant. Safe and hidden behind the curtain, they experienced the spiritual world as one would immediately after death. For three and a half days they would lay hidden and apparently dead behind the curtain of the Holy

---

[92] John 11

[93] Rudolf Steiner, *The Gospel of John*, GA 103, SteinerBooks, 1984

of the Holies until the hierophant called them back to their dying bodies.

The Eleusinian mystai lay as if dead within the Telesterion for 3.5 days. Now compare this to chapter 11 of The Gospel of John and the raising of Lazarus. Three and a half days is the same time period in which Lazarus was "dead". We can see that Christ was the hierophant. When the high priests heard about this initiation of Lazarus taking place public and not within the Holy of the Holies, they held an emergency session. We read beginning in *John* chapter 11 verse 47, "Then the chief priests and the Pharisees called a meeting of the Sanhedrin. 'What are we accomplishing?' they asked. 'Here is this man performing many signs. If we let him go on like this, everyone will believe in him, and then the Romans will come and take away both our temple and our nation.' Then one of them, named Caiaphas, who was high priest that year, spoke up, 'You know nothing at all! You do not realize that it is better for you that one man dies for the people than that the whole nation perishes.' He did not say this on his own (out of his own personality), but as high priest that year he prophesied that Jesus would die for the Jewish nation, and not only for that nation but also for the scattered children of God, to bring them together and make them one. So, from that day on they plotted to take his life."[94] The old law of the temple required that anyone who reveals its secrets must forfeit their life. Did Christ knowingly force this resolution by the priests who were responsible for temple initiations? What were the theologians of the coming centuries to make of this? With Lazarus, did Christ bring to an end this form of initiation? Did he also bring to an end the form of initiation from sitting under a tree such as the fig or bodhi tree?[95]

In ancient times, one was selected by the priests to join a mystery center. Bloodline played a major role. Later, in Hellenistic times, it became one's initiative to participate. As individualism grew out of the old tribalism, so did the desire for an ecstatic, spiritual experience grow as an egotistical personal lifegoal. Eventually, conquerors demanded to be initiated. The secrecy was betrayed. Formerly, only one who underwent certain tests would be allowed to learn something of them. The neophyte was always told "only as

---

[94] John 11:47-54, NIV
[95] Mark 11:12-25

much as was appropriate for his or her intellectual, spiritual, and moral faculties. This had to be so, for when properly used, the higher insights are the key to a power which must lead to misuse in the hands of the unprepared."[96]

With the growth of individualism out of tribalism came also both egoism and egotism. To combat these, "Oh Man, Know Thou Thyself" was written over the entrance to Delphi's Temple to Apollo and its Mystery School. Egotism brought pride and unreal images of one's character. It was believed that only one who was truthful and humble could enter the spiritual world.

Jewish Mysticism

The Essenes and the Dead Sea Scrolls

At the time of Christ, there existed three main sects of Judaism: the Sadducees, the Pharisees, and the Essenes. As an outcome of the 70 CE Jewish Uprising, Rome banished all Jews from the Roman state of Judah. This included all three sects. As the Roman soldiers drove the Jews into exile, some hid their treasured books and scrolls in these caves. Here they remained

---

[96] Rudolf Steiner, *Cosmic Memory*, 1904, GA 11

until, by chance, Bedouin shepherds Muhammed edh-Dhib, Jum'a Muhammed, and Khalil Musa, found some of the scrolls in different caves between November 1946 and February 1947.

Later in 1947, the original scrolls, seven in total, caught the attention of Dr. John C. Trever, of the American Schools of Oriental Research (ASOR). But, in March of 1948, the Arab–Israeli War broke out. By the end of 1948, no one had been able to locate the original cave where the fragments had been found. Safety remained an issue. Finally, on January 28, 1949, Cave 1 was rediscovered by Arab Legion Captain Akkash el-Zebn and a United Nations observer, Captain Phillipe Lippens.

Many early Christian communities continued to practice Jewish customs. By 70 CE, some early Christian texts likely existed within the Jewish communities around Jerusalem. Biblical scholar and professor, Robert Eisenman, has argued that some Dead Sea Scrolls describe the early Christian community.[97] Therein are

---

[97] Robert Eisenman, *James, the Brother of Jesus: The Key to Unlocking the Secrets of Early Christianity and the*

described activities of Paul the Apostle as well as the brother of Jesus, James the Just. These accounts correspond to events recorded in the New Testament.

Soul Cleanliness and the Dead Sea Scrolls

Baptism was well described in the Dead Sea Scrolls. Baptism in water was also an established rite within the Mysteries. Before entering a holy place, one should 'come clean', to confess one's sins, so as not to pollute the air, that is, the atmosphere where holy rituals and burnt offerings were to take place. As we've heard, esoteric truths existed on many levels. Water was symbolic of life and used for its cleansing capacity. The seas were salty because water could combine with such earthy elements, carry them away, and then, through evaporation, rise towards the heavens to be cleansed itself from where it could resume this cycle.

The sins that baptism could cleanse were seen as sins of the flesh. It was these that John the Baptist sought to cleanse so that individuals could be prepared to receive the Holy Spirit. Matthew 3 and Luke 3 both describe John the

---

Dead Sea Scrolls. 1st American ed. New York: Viking, 1997

Baptist's statement, "I baptize you with water for repentance. But after me comes one who is more powerful than I, whose sandals I am not worthy to carry. He will baptize you with the Holy Spirit and fire."[98]

We find in Dead Sea Scroll Manuscript A, Fragment 3 the words "the Holy Spirit settling upon His Messiah." This passage compares itself to Isaiah 11:2 "The Spirit of the Lord would settle on Him" and to John 1:32 where we read, "John also testified, 'I saw the Spirit coming down from heaven like a dove, and it remained on him' [Intl Standard Version] or "and it abode upon him [King James Version]." For the Gnostics, to 'settle upon' was not the same as to 'integrate with'. In any case, the Holy Spirit would only arrive at the Baptism of the Messiah; it would not be present at the birth of the physical body. In the Nag Hammadi Gnostic text, *Paraphrases of Shem*, Jesus describes his own full immersion baptism, "Then shall I come down ... to the water. And whirlpools of water and flames of fire will rise up against me. Then I shall come up from the water, having put on the light of Faith and the unquenchable fire, in order that through my

---

[98] Matthew 3:11, NIV and Luke 3:16, NIV

help the power of the Spirit may cross over ..."[99]

Basilides was an Alexandrian and a Gnostic whose teacher had been Peter's disciple Glaucius plus he claimed written inheritance from the Apostle Mattias who had replaced Judas Iscariot. Basilides wrote about the Baptism of Jesus for his followers, "So from the sphere of the Seven [perhaps Seven Elohim or perhaps the seven planets] the Light ... descended upon Jesus, the son of Mary, and he was illuminated and kindled by the Light that shone upon him."[100] Again, we find that the Early Christians did not see Christ-on-earth as extending back to the birth of Jesus.

The Ending of Christianity's Esoteric Roots

As the unworthy and the unclean gradually debased the former glory of the Mysteries, the spiritual world itself was forced to withdraw. Over a thousand-year period, from roughly 700

---

[99] *Paraphrase of Shem*, Codex 7, translated by Andrew Welburn, *The Beginnings of Christianity*, Floris Press, 1991

[100] Hippolytus declares Basilides to be a heretic in *Refutation of Heresies* VII 26:8.

BCE to roughly 300 CE, the Mysteries gradually fell into decadence.

From Julian the Apostate to Justinian the Great

Roman emperor Julian the Apostate (331-363 CE) tried to restore the Mysteries to their former glory, but it was too late. Julian would end up being assassinated by his own Christian soldiers when he sought a Persian initiation during his conquest there.[101] After Julian, both the powers of state and the powers of religion sought to destroy this heritage so that no future Julian might try again thereby splitting the connection of the Church with the Imperial state. With these two joined, the Church was empowered to destroy what it deemed to be the heresies. Even the esoteric streams within Christianity came under scrutiny and attack.

Emperors Theodosius I (347 – 395 CE) and Justinian (482 – 565 CE) lent their support, even troops, to the destruction of the ancient

---

[101] Adrian Murdock, *The Last Pagan, Julian the Apostate and the Death of the Ancient World*, Inner Traditions, 2008

mysteries, their temples, and their literary history.[102]

Two days after he had arrived in Constantinople in 380 CE to be crowned emperor, Theodosius expelled the non-Nicene bishop, Demophilus as Patriarch of Constantinople. The Church bowed to his demand to replace him with Gregory of Nazianzus, one of the Cappadocian Fathers. Next, Theodosius appointed Meletius Patriarch

Figure 10 Justinian, mosaic, Basilica of San Vitale, Ravenna, sixth century

---

[102] John B. Bury, *History of the Later Roman Empire from the Death of Theodosius I to the Death of Justinian*, vol. 1, Dover, 1923

of Antioch. In that same year, Theodosius issued his "Cunctos populos" decree that declared the Nicene Trinitarian Christianity to be the only legitimate imperial religion and the only one entitled to call itself Catholic. This decree, known as the Edict of Thessalonica, ended official state support or tolerance for the traditional polytheist religions and customs. Theodosius concludes all other Christians are "foolish madmen".[103]

History records how in 64 CE, under Nero, Christians were brutally persecuted in Rome. Next, under Theodosius I, the tables were turned so that the Christian authorities persecuted those of the old Roman religion. To consolidate the diversity under the flag of Catholicism, Theodosius removed all non-Nicene Christians from church office. He tolerated no other religion by criminalizing any who did not enforce laws against polytheism. He punished all who practiced witchcraft. He broke up long established pagan associations and converted former holidays of pagan religions into workdays. He closed Roman temples and encouraged mob attacks on

---

103 https://sourcebooks.fordham.edu/source/theodcodexvi.asp accessed 9August2018

pagan temples whose endowments he confiscated. Only Orthodox Christianity would be tolerated by the state under Theodosius.

A hundred years later, Justinian would complete this annihilation of the ancient world. Using his concept of symphony between church and state, Justinian held the "conviction that the unity of the Empire presupposed unity of faith, and it appeared to him obvious that this faith could only be the orthodox (Nicaean)."[104] Because of his siding with Orthodoxy in the remaining theological battles, and because of his rebuilding in 537 of the basilica Hagia Sophia (or Holy Wisdom), he was bequeathed sainthood. The previous basilica was destroyed by mob during the Nika Riots of 532 that sought to oust the brutal emperor Justinian. The mob came about when partisans of rival chariot racing factions in Constantinople united against Justinian in a revolt. They sought to replace him with the senator Hypatius, who was a nephew of the late emperor Anastasius. While the crowd was rioting in the streets, Justinian considered fleeing the capital by sea, but decided to stay,

---

[104] https://en.wikipedia.org/wiki/Justinian_I accessed 9August2018

apparently on the prompting of his wife, Theodora, who refused to leave. In the next two days, he ordered the brutal suppression of the riots by his generals Belisarius and Mundus. Procopius relates that 30,000 unarmed civilians were killed in the Hippodrome. On Theodora's insistence, and apparently against his own judgment, Justinian had Anastasius' nephews executed.

In the third and fourth century, the leaders of Christianity, many of whom had been trained by initiates, struggled with what Christianity was to mean to future human evolution. With materialism growing strong, they knew that concepts associated with reincarnation were vanishing. Christianity needed to stress the importance of each life, especially one's current life. It seemed obvious that the former attainment of knowledge was no longer possible for most. The idea of a path of faith in addition to knowledge began to take root.

Gnosticism when blended with egoism became elitist. Their members were often accused of pride in knowledge, a pride that lacked love. As egoism infiltrated Gnosticism, it rendered it untenable as a Christian knowledge-based path that could apply to all people equally. The charge of elitism fueled a campaign to oust Gnosticism from Christianity. It was likely that with the rise of egotism, many Gnostics did indeed feel superior to the uneducated masses, but the path of Gnosticism was also supposed to be a path of humility in which one rose in consciousness step-by-step to eventual union with God through Christ. The Orthodox raised the issue of knowledge without love citing 1 Corinthians, "We know that 'We all possess knowledge.' But knowledge puffs up while love builds up. Those who think they know something do not yet know as they ought to know. But whoever loves God is known by God."[105]

As we've seen, Gnosticism was not so much a path of outer knowledge, but of inner knowledge. It would have agreed with the Delphic saying "Oh Man, Know Thou Thyself!" With each step towards inner knowledge, the seeker had to overcome something within. Such were the steps of soul purification, steps towards perfection. The Perfect felt compassion for those left behind following initiation. The knowledge was to be used not to leave the cycle of reincarnation, but to help

[105] 1 Cor 8:1-3, NIV

all advance through knowledge to conscious love. But pride did enter with egoism that came with the development of the human intellect during these centuries.

Thus, the emphasis moved from knowledge to love. Upon this basis, not knowledge, Christian leaders felt Christianity could fulfill its mission. They reasoned that the contemporary human mind could grasp only the ponderable but since God was imponderable, faith was needed for this new religion. Moreover, as Christianity had fulfilled the expectations of the ancient Mysteries as well as the prophecies of the Jewish mystics, something totally new could now enter human evolution. After all, the new commandment was to love one another as I (Christ) have loved you.[106]

This impetus towards the new led to the justification, however brutal, for the destruction of the old, especially everything pagan. This was done by using the label "heresy." It fell upon each and every Christianity that did not break with this past. In a triumph for materialism after the fourth century, Greek metaphysics, magic, witchery,

---

[106] This commandment appears in John 13:34 and John 15:12 and Romans 13:8

and anything esoteric or occult wore the heresy label. Eventually, these became associated with evil. This association of the occult with evil persists even in our times.

Thus, the old must fade away and be replaced by the new. This was portrayed in Grunewald's Crucifixion within the Isenheim Altarpiece (1512 – 1516) where St. John is saying to the crucified savior, "He must increase, and I must decrease."

Figure 11 Detail, Crucifixion, Grunewald, "He must increase, and I must decrease!"

Florentine art revived Neo-Platonism. In doing so, the artists sought how to depict scenes from Greek mythology as forerunners for events during the time of Christ on the earth. With this renewed enthusiasm for Greek philosophy, mythology, and art, Greek statues were excavated from underground in much of Italy. Texts from the East flowed into Italy adding excitement to the rebirth of Knowledge. In addition to the texts, was mysticism also reborn in Florentine circles?

The mysticism that existed in early Christianity had continued underground, out of view of the Church. When the Church had become so weak in the fifteenth century, mystical practices, especially those related to alchemy and science, were tolerated if kept out of public view. A network of astronomers, professors, mathematicians, and natural philosophers in sixteenth century formed the "Invisible College". Members included Johannes Kepler, Georg Joachim Rheticus, John Dee and Tycho Brahe. When refounded in 1660, it then became known as the Royal Society and it still exists today. Among its members was Robert Boyle who wrote: "the cornerstones of the Invisible College do now and then honour me with their company ..."[107]

---

[107] Robert Lomas, *The Invisible College*, Headline, 2003

The Early Heresy Hunters

Irenaeus of Gaul (today Lyon, France)

By the third generation of Christian leaders, the evolution of the various Christianities had become a serious issue. Just as St. Paul had confronted St. Peter about converting new Christians through Jewish traditions, these various Christianities bickered about differences in theology. Some claimed other Christians were wrong and thus heretics. Some were appalled by elitism within the Christian Gnostics and other knowledge-based groups. Many sought to establish Christianity as the new Mystery while silencing the old.

These new leaders took on a role that would later be called Heresy Hunter by historians. One of the first of these was Irenaeus of Lyons (140 – 202) in Gaul (today, France). As author of *Against Heresies*,[108] he battled all other Christian streams that he felt had drifted from the true faith. Irenaeus had been taught by

---

[108] The actual title of this book is *On the Detection and Overthrow of the So-Called Gnosis*, appeared between 174 and 189. It took aim at Biblical exegesis by Gnostics such as Valentinus. Until Nag Hammadi, what historians knew about Gnosticism was based on this book. It has been shown that Irenaeus misrepresented Gnostic teachings.

Polycarp who had been taught by the apostle John, the son of Zebedee (not the author of John's Gospel for that is John the Evangelist). Polycarp was one of (at least) three acknowledged Apostolic Fathers of the Catholic Church (the other two being Clement of Rome and Ignatius of Antioch).[109] Polycarp was a companion of Papias who was a "hearer of John"[110] and a correspondent of Ignatius of Antioch. Irenaeus was certain that any other Christianity that differed significantly from what he had been taught, because his teachers were directly from one of the apostles, must be wrong and therefore a heresy. It did not matter that others also claimed a direct line from one of the apostles.

While Irenaeus condemned a practice of merging Christianity themes and holidays with pagan ones to convince its peoples to convert, he could not grasp how each of the twelve (or more) apostolic versions of Christianity could also be right. His "I'm right and you're wrong" approach within theology rested on the power

---

[109] Others such as Origen could be considered a father of the Church, but he was denounced two centuries later as a heretic.

[110] Note the term "hearer" and its use within Manichaeism discussed later

of his direct line to one of twelve of the apostles. He may have been aware, but did not condemn, the work of scribes who altered sacred texts perhaps under their leader's wish, to better fit their flock's outlook. Bart Ehrman and other scholars have shown how this happened to six[111] of the letters attributed to St. Paul where insertions were made altering theological positions. For example, to keep women out of Church affairs and the priesthood, words were added to Paul's letters such as 1 Corinthians 14.[112] Those advocating for the theology of Irenaeus, a proto-Orthodox, may also have been involved in altering sacred text to better fit their theology according to religious historian Bart Ehrman.[113]

Irenaeus' teacher Polycarp, soon after the time Anicetus had been installed as Bishop of Rome (roughly 160), journeyed there to discuss

---

[111] Drake Williams, "Paul the Apostle, Critical Issues," *The Lexham Bible Dictionary*, John D. Barry, et. al., eds Lexham Press, 2016; Also see https://crossexamined.org/paul-write-thirteen-letters-attributed/ accessed 28Jun2018

[112] Bart Ehrman, *Forgery and Counterforgery*, Oxford University Press, 2012, also see https://en.wikipedia.org/wiki/Women_in_Church_history

[113] IBID

theological differences that existed between Asia and Rome. Anicetus' primary concern was when to set the Easter festival. Polycarp had followed the eastern practice of celebrating Easter according to when Passover was observed. Anicetus followed the western practice of celebrating the feast on the first Sunday after the first full moon after the Spring equinox.[114] Anicetus wanted to excommunicate all of those in Asia who set Easter to be coincident with the 14th of Nisan, that is, with the setting of the Jewish Passover.[115] Polycarp, a fellow Syrian, realizing

---

[114] By following the sun-based calendar of Julius Caesar, the Roman Church's setting of Easter began to drift from the moon-based Jewish calendar. This drift became severe by the sixteenth century when in 1582, when Pope Gregory XIII sought to correct and stop the drift with a new calendar known today as the Gregorian Calendar. See https://en.wikipedia.org/wiki/Gregorian_calendar for more.

[115] Rome championed a split from the Jewish moon-based calendar for the Roman sun-based Julian calendar. As such Easter was to be set on the first Sunday following the first full moon that followed the spring equinox. All this became further confused, especially for modern laypeople, when the Julian calendar was reset to the Gregorian calendar. Calendar drift had moved festivals from the equinoxes and solstices to the 25th of their month so when the shift happened, the 25th was retained. Also, when Rome put down the Jewish revolt of 70 CE, Christians sought to

that this excommunication would apply to him, talked Anicetus out of this resolution! Here we can see the beginning of the use of power to establish dogmas to rule over knowledge. Incidentally, when Victor was Bishop of Rome (189 – 199), Irenaeus needs to repeat this drama around excommunication regarding Easter all over again. We also see that at this time, being labeled a heretic meant (merely) excommunication. Those excommunicated often would set up their own church with its own See (Pope) and carryon their brand of Christianity.

Hippolytus of Rome

Following Irenaeus, his two students Hippolytus of Rome (170-235) and Tertullian of Carthage (155 – 240) take up the mantle as chief heresy hunters. Of Hippolytus's many works, the one most influential to heresy hunting was *Refutation of All Heresies*.[116] This work is divided into ten books.

Book 1 was known as the Philosophoumena (Greek: Φιλοσοφούμενα "philosophical

---

distance their religion so it could not be accused of being an offshoot of Judaism.

116 https://en.wikipedia.org/wiki/Refutation_of_All_Heresies

teachings"). It appeared in several larger church-teaching manuscripts. It offers a summary of the thought of various ancient Greek philosophers. Hippolytus's arguments lead to the conclusion that the works of Pythagoras, Plato, and Aristotle are heretical! He also outlines the philosophies of the Brahmins of India, Zamolxis of Thrace, and the Celtic Druids! He reasons why these pagan as well as Gnostic-Christian beliefs were heretical. Until the Nag Hammadi texts were found, this book was the historical source for information about these heresies.

Books 2 and 3 have not yet been found. Books 4 – 10 were recovered in 1842 in a manuscript at Mount Athos. Book 4 deals with various diviners, magicians, and astrologers. This book concludes by trying to prove a link between Pythagoras and his mystery school and the Gnostic branches of Valentinus and Simon Magus. In doing so, Hippolytus shines the heresy beacon on all of the ancient Mysteries and all Hellenistic philosophies. This became the position of the Church of Rome. It helped to drive out in the West this historical knowledge until it could return at the start of the Renaissance.

5. The Battle for the Soul of Christianity

As the second century was coming to a close, regional churches each with their own doctrinal foundation and some with their own See existed across Christendom. Without a consensus on theology and doctrine, discord grew. History then provided two prolific writers to record the struggles for the Soul of Christianity. Within these writers' texts are revealed the essence of the theological debates that raged as the second century came to an end and the third began.

Of great concern was the meaning and reality to each member of the Holy Trinity. Its corollary was to whom of the Trinity was humanity's direct relationship? Was it foremost to the Son, or to Holy Spirit, or to the Father? To whom should we pray: one of these or to our guardian angel? Did the Father beget the Son? Is the Son subordinate to the Father? What is the role (or the point) of the Holy Spirit? If these three are not the same single God, then might they be Gods at different levels? Are they equals? Are they made of the same or of different substances?

At this time, with the surging of materialism, an angelic being might have remarked how much the devil of deceit must be enjoying his work during this period of history.

Origen (or Origenes)

With over 2,000 treatises to his name, Origen of Alexandria (184-253) is called "the greatest genius the early church ever produced"[117] and "the first major Christian theologian."[118] Of particular interest to us here regarding Origen's theology is his notion of the "pre-existence" of souls. Not every scholar has concluded that this entails reincarnation, but for most scholars it does. Origen's serenity leads back through the Neoplatonists to the ancient Mystery wisdom.

In his feelings for *Sophia*, i.e., for knowledge, Origen translated the Old Testament to provide six interlinear versions called the *Hexapla* (from the Greek word for 'sixfold'). He arranged for six parallel columns for

---

[117] John Anthony McGuckin, *The Westminster Handbook to Origen*, Westminster John Knox Press, 2004

[118] Edward Moore, "Origen of Alexandria (185—254 C.E.)", *Internet Encyclopedia of Philosophy, A Peer-Reviewed Academic Resource*, 2014 and https://www.iep.utm.edu/origen-of-alexandria/ accessed 2Jul2018

comparative study. The columns contained the original Hebrew, a transliteration into Greek letters, followed by the Septuagint,[119] and finally three Greek translations that had been done by other Christian scholars. Origen was truly a great scholar.

Origen's Theology

Origen, as translated from his Greek, wrote on the Trinity as follows, "The God and Father, who holds the universe together, is superior to every being that exists, for he imparts to each one from his own existence that which each one is. The Son, being less than the Father, is superior to rational creatures alone (for he is second to the Father); the Holy Spirit is still less, and dwells within the saints alone. So that in this way the power of the Father is greater than that of the Son and of the Holy Spirit, and that of the Son is more than that of the Holy Spirit, and in turn the power of the Holy Spirit exceeds that of every other holy being."[120]

---

[119] Greek translation of the Old Testament from the original Hebrew, see https://en.wikipedia.org/wiki/Septuagint

[120] Origen, *Fragment 9* (Koetschau), translated by Butterworth, 1966

Declaring Origen a Heretic

Until the start of the fifth century, Origen was regarded as the bastion of orthodoxy.[121] At the same time, however, many commonalities exist between Origen's theology and that of the so-called heretic Arius.[122] (Arius will be discussed in more detail later).

As the fifth century dawned, metaphysical thoughts had become associated with heresy. Theophilus, Patriarch of Alexandria, condemned Origen's works in 399. His control over Epiphanius, the Bishop of Cyprus, caused him to call for a Synod in order to condemn Origen. Historian Socrates Scholasticus wrote that Theophilus had 'deluded Epiphanius' to turn against Origen. Theophilus led an army against monks who supported Origen. His army burned the monk's dwellings and ill-treated those captured. Because of this, he was summoned to apologize to the synod. Many wanted to remove Theophilus from his post as Patriarch. The Synod of the Oak, as it

---

[121] Roger E. Olson, *The Story of Christian Theology: Twenty Centuries of Tradition & Reform*, InterVarsity Press, 1999

[122] Rowan Williams, *Arius: Heresy and Tradition*, William B. Eerdmans Publishing Company, 2001

was called, became the Council of Alexandria of 403 CE.

Knowing how to deal with such things, Theophilus stacked the deck in his favor. The council took place in Alexandria where he was Patriarch. Although summoned to come alone, he arrived with 29 bishops that supported him. Also known to use money to win votes and favors, he came with a good deal of money and all sorts of gifts.[123] And he arrived with his nephew and successor Cyril to teach him 'the ropes.' We will learn more about Cyril later.

Living in luxury, Theophilus took his lodgings in one of the imperial palaces. Here he met with adversaries of Chrysostom (John Chrysostom was the Patriarch (Pope) of Constantinople and considered his main opponent). By the time this council was convened, Theophilus had the votes to escape his own denunciation and instead to swung this to condemn his opposition on false grounds. The Christian church was sliding rapidly into moral depravity.

---

[123] Socrates Scholasticus, *Ecclesiastical History,* Book 6, see https://www.ccel.org/ccel/schaff/npnf202.ii.ix.xi.html

On the issue of declaring Origen to be a heretic, Theotimus, Bishop of Scythia, stood to address the puppet Epiphanius and the council. According to the historian Socrates Scholasticus, Theotimus spoke these words, "'I neither choose, Epiphanius, to insult the memory of one who ended his life piously long ago; nor dare I be guilty of so impious an act, as that of condemning what our predecessors did not reject: and especially when I know of no evil doctrine contained in Origen's books.' Having said this, he brought forward one of that author's works, and reading a few passages therefrom, showed that the sentiments propounded were in perfect accordance with the orthodox faith. He then added, 'Those who speak evil of these writings are unconsciously casting dishonor upon the sacred volume whence their principles are drawn.' Such was the reply which Theotimus, a bishop, celebrated for his piety and rectitude of life, made to Epiphanius."[124]

Because Origen had been so popular, Pope Theophilus felt the need to go on a campaign to denounce Origen. Theophilus called him

---

124 https://www.ccel.org/ccel/schaff/npnf202.ii.ix.xiii.html

"the hydra of all heresies!" But Eastern Christianity was not so apt to condemn their philosophical hero.[125] Origen had been revered as one of the greatest of all Christian teachers, especially beloved by monks. Both the so-called heretics as well as the orthodox theologians had been followers in the tradition Origen.[126] With the condemnation of Origen, the existing split between East and West that commenced with the Council of Nicaea, 325, widened. This would continue until the Great Schism of 1054.

Christian Theology from Origen to Tertullian

With the Mysteries having fallen into decadence and materialism taking its place, Tertullian and Origen exemplified the theological crisis of their time. As Origen was revered in the East, Tertullian slowly became a theological giant for the West. While Origen sought his foundation in Greek metaphysics, Tertullian carried his realism to the verge of materialism. He despised the metaphysics of Greek philosophy, especially Plato and

---

[125] Roger E. Olson, *The Story of Christian Theology: Twenty Centuries of Tradition & Reform*, InterVarsity Press, 1999

[126] IBID

Aristotle. He called these and the other Greek philosophers the patriarchal forefathers of the heretics. His distrust of Greek philosophers sinks into Orthodox Christianity to become their position in the fifth century.

Tertullian, is called the "founder of Western theology"[127] in part because his work on the Trinity was accepted. The heights to which Tertullian rose for the Western Church, Origen rose similarly for the Eastern Church. And while Origen's massive theological treatise *On the First Principles*, laid out the foundations of Christian theology that persisted for centuries following his death, Tertullian's apologetics against all forms of paganism and also Judaism plus his call for a whole reorganization of human life on a Christian basis prepared the foundation for the vicious cleansing of the heresies to come. While Origen retained the ancient humility, Tertullian exemplified the rise in egotism when he lashed out at his opponents calling them such things as blind, perverse, or utterly stupid.[128] Tertullian's

---

[127] Justo Gonzáles, *The Story of Christianity, Vol 1, The Early Church to the Dawn of the Reformation*, HarperOne, 2010

[128] Tertullian used "caeci", "perversissime", "stultissime" in his *Adversus Praxean* 22, 23, 28.

persuasive personality led Christianity forward without a need to acknowledge what was now in the past.

Tertullian's Theology

The theology of Tertullian (155-240), Treis Hypostases – Homoousios, meaning "three persons - one substance," caused divisive debates about the Trinity. These bitter debates led to Ecumenical Councils that were meant to settle such disputes. For Tertullian, the Son was subordinate to the Father. But for many other Trinitarians, the Father, the Son, and Holy Spirit were all equal. Some claimed they were essentially the same, just different aspects of one spiritual being.

Tertullian strongly defended the Pentecostal-like nature of Montanism. Unfortunately, his work in defense of it, *De ecstasi* has been lost. Montanus had been a priest of Apollo perhaps as part of a Mystery Center in Phrygia. Montanus met and converted to Christianity in 135. Something more happened, perhaps an initiation, because soon thereafter Montanus said that the Paraclete[129] spoke through him. We will see that Mani had a similar claim a few

---

[129] It means advocate or helper. In Christianity, the term "paraclete" typically refers to the Holy Spirit.

decades later. This raised the question, "does the Holy Spirit remain active with humans?" Or was Pentecost the one and only action of the Holy Spirit?

Of Montanus' flock, several claimed the Holy Spirit spoke through them. Two of these were women known as Priscilla and Maximilla. Together these three proclaimed *The New Prophecy*. Montanism and its New Prophecy spread in Christendom causing much alarm within the Orthodox. Similarly, to modern Pentecostal Christianity,[130] members of different congregations also became speakers for the Holy Spirit. In Carthage, North Africa and Tertullian's hometown, Montanism was tolerated. To make this acceptable, a council of elders was formed to whom the role of determining what was genuine revelation and what was not.[131] In order to honestly perform such a role, these elders must have had some clairvoyant sight.

---

[130] See https://en.wikipedia.org/wiki/Pentecostalism

[131] William Tabbernee, *Prophets and Gravestones: An Imaginative History of Montanists and Other Early Christians*, Hendrickson, 2009

Who is the Father God of the Trinity?

Marcion

During 207 and 208 Tertullian wrote five books against Marcion (85 – 160). These are his most comprehensive and extensive works. They clearly offer the proto-Orthodox view that Gnosticism was a heresy. Marcion had claimed that Jehovah or Yahweh[132] was an important god but not the same as the Father God referred to by Christ-Jesus. Described in his book *Antitheses*, Marcion based this on the very different characteristics of the God of the Old Testament and the Father God Christ refers to in the New Testament. An example of his struggle to resolve this is found in the expressions "an eye for an eye and a tooth for a tooth" compared to the god of mercy, forgiveness, and love of the New Testament.

Marcion agrees with Plato and the Gnostics that a lesser god than the Father created the physical world. He uses their term for this god,

---

[132] Hebrew did not begin to use vowels until about 400. The Hebrew word יהוה is literally translated as YHWH which can be read as Jehovah or Yahweh. Only once a year was the high priest allowed to speak this name and only within the Holy of the Holies, behind the closed curtain. YHWH in esoteric Christan lore refers to one of the seven Elohim.

Demiurge.[133] Marcion was worried about materialism and its ability to pollute his Christ-based theology. He thus denied a physical and bodily birth, death, and resurrection for the Son God, Christ. It is not clear from what documentation remains if Marcion distinguished between Christ and Jesus, but it seems likely that he did so in order to have had the physical vehicle for the Christ ready for use from the time of baptism to his death on Golgotha. Although he would become labeled a heretic, it was his action to select authentic books for a canon that led bishops of the proto-Orthodox to do similarly two centuries later.

The Struggle to Understand the Christian Trinity

Theological concepts themselves have evolved over great historical periods. A trinitarian concept arose during the era of the ancient Egyptian (c. 3000 – 750 BC), Chaldean, Assyrian, and Babylonian times. We see trinity in the myth of Osiris, Isis, and Horace. Other gods, such as Set, of course exist, but these three comprise a trinity that can also be found

---

[133] The term, Demiurge, can be traced back to 360 BC in Plato's *Timaeus*, where the demiurge is described as the creator of the physical universe.

in the human soul, namely the capacities for thinking, feeling, and willing. Prior to this period, duality reigned as the predominate theological concept. Polarities were explored as a way towards knowledge. This was seen in the ancient Persian (c. 5000 – 3000 BC) mythology with the polarity battles of Ormudz (sun light) and Ahriman (darkness). And before the Persian era was the ancient Indian culture whose theological concept was based on unity.

These myths resided within a culture's oral tradition. For northern Europe, the Norse mythology had the trinity of Odin, Frigg, and their Baldur. In these myths, it was the son, Baldur, rather than the father, Odin, who was the god slain (by Set in Egyptian, Loki in Norse myth).

From northern Europe also came what is known today as the Grimm's Fairy tales. In these stories there is frequently a fading-away King or father. The queen or stepmother is present but also fading. The tale often has a princess who endures hardships or falls into a deep and long-lasting sleep. A prince or even a fool comes along and rescues the princess. Typically, the male represented the spirit while the female represented the soul. The prince, like Horace, represents something new in spirit. This is similar to St. Paul calling the risen Christ, the second or last Adam.[134]

Hellenistic philosophers spoke trinitarian terms: monad, dyad, and world-soul. The Christians who followed spoke of Father, Son, and Holy Spirit. Consistent with their times and as spirit beings only, these three received male labels. Other beings of the heavenly hierarchy such as archangels were seen as androgynous but typically were given male names, for example Gabriel.

Of the different theologies that arose from the twelve Christianites, the Battle Over the Trinity became the first bloodletting. Although it is difficult to grasp today why such questions could lead to such battles, it shows how difficult it is for us today to put ourselves into these former times.

The fought-over trinitarian questions were:

- Are these three Gods equal?
- Did the Father beget the Son?
- Where did the Holy Spirit come from?

---

[134] 1 Corinthians 15:45, "The first man Adam was made a living ***soul***; the last Adam was made a quickening ***spirit***", KJV

- Were they all in existence from before "the Beginning," the Creation?
- Were they on different spiritual levels?
- Were they of the same substance?
- How do each of the Trinity reflect within the human being?

We can see how materialism had infiltrated Christian theology when the question of substance was debated. Bear in mind, bodily substance implies the members of the Trinity had some existence similar to that of a physical body. Although they may have created the physical world, they existed "above" the physical according to the trinitarian philosophy of their day.

6. Formation of the New Testament Canon

If Faith was to become uniform, the leaders of the Church realized that of the many books circulating among the Christian communities, there was a need to bless a selection of these. Only those theologically approved texts would be allowed to elucidate the faith. Only those books that were clearly divinely inspired should become the Canon. Thus did Athanasius of Alexandria write in 367, "I will employ the example of Luke the evangelist and say myself: Inasmuch as certain people have attempted to set in order for themselves the so-called apocryphal books and to mix these with the *divinely inspired* Scripture, about which we are convinced *it is just as those who were eyewitnesses* from the beginning and assistants of the Word handed down to our ancestors, it seemed good to me, because I have been urged by genuine brothers and sisters and instructed from the beginning, to *set forth in order the books that are canonized*, transmitted, and *believed to be divine*, so that those who have been deceived might condemn the persons who led them astray, and those who have remained pure might rejoice to be reminded."

Requirements to be an Author of Scripture

What was required of those near to one or another of the Apostles to be able to write their gospel? Was the divine inspiration through the Apostle or through the book's author? Did the author go to the divine fountain of wisdom or did the divine take over their body and write the texts through them (critics asked, "could God write in Greek")?

How did readers know that a given text was divinely inspired? Or was a text authentic?

Some scholars such as Delbert Burkett[135] have concluded that the gospels evolved without divine inspiration through four stages:

1. First there was an oral tradition that included sayings and various stories about Jesus.
2. Next, the oral traditions began to be written down in collections
3. Then written collections and oral traditions were combined into "proto-gospels"
4. Finally, the authors of our four Gospels drew on these proto gospels to produce the gospels of Matthew, Mark, Luke and John.

But such books would not have passed the "divinely inspired" test by those whose initiations granted them such insights. Such a perspective fails to recognize the "truth-on-many-levels," i.e., the mystery inherent in the gospels.

---

[135] Burkett, Delbert, *An introduction to the New Testament and the origins of Christianity*, Cambridge University Press, 2002

Were such authors also Christian Initiates – is this what was meant by Paul when he wrote, "For we speak a wisdom among the initiated, a wisdom not of this aeon, nor of the world-rulers of this aeon who are passing away. We speak a wisdom of God in a mystery, an occult wisdom which God ordained before the aeons for our glory, and which none of the world-rulers of this aeon knows."[136] [the eternal realm of Ideas was for Plato a region of the aeons. But in "region" I've used a word that denotes spatial dimension. Aeon could also denote types of consciousness or eras of time. For example, as the sun passes through the zodiac, we can conceive of this in both spatial and temporal concepts as well as in changes of cosmic consciousness.]

Recognized Scripture Authors

Paul's letters circulated among the early communities (Colossians 4:16; 1 Thessalonians 5:27). Peter recognized Paul's writings as consciously written from spiritual sight, writing "Bear in mind that our Lord's patience means salvation, just as our dear brother Paul also wrote you with the wisdom that God gave him. He writes the same way in all his letters,

---

[136] 1 Cor. 2:6-8

speaking in them of these matters. His letters contain some things that are hard to understand [mystical], which ignorant and unstable people distort, as they do the other Scriptures, to their own destruction."[137] (2 Peter 3:15-16). Here Peter alludes to the misunderstandings of the mysteries of scripture by those whose knowledge is not yet sufficiently prepared.

The writers of the four gospels likely were scribes as well as students of their apostolic teacher. What they learned in this oral tradition from their teachers we can only imagine. We presume in this book, that these students did not write only from what they heard. Rather, they took part in the new Christian initiation and therefore could write from this higher perspective. As inspired writing, what is recorded is said to have multiple levels of meaning. Further, those who were responsible for selecting which of the many books in circulation within the many Christian communities had likely progressed to some introductory level of initiation. A soul mood in the author of reverence and

[137] 2 Peter 3:15-16

faithfulness to the divine was essential. No egoism was permissible.

Letters by other church leaders help to understand what else was circulating. Clement of Rome mentioned at least eight New Testament books (CE 95). Ignatius of Antioch listed about seven books (CE 115). Polycarp acknowledged 15 books (CE 108). His student, Irenaeus, listed 21 books (CE 185). Then Hippolytus recognized 22 books (CE 170-235) as divinely inspired. Not all of the books now in the New Testament were so easily identified. Hebrews, James, 2 Peter, 2 John, and 3 John underwent considerable controversy before being accepted.

Books that did not make it into the canon but were used by Fathers of the Church include *Barnabas, Didache, I Clement, Revelation of Peter, The Shepherd, The Gospel According to the Hebrews, The Gospel of the Egyptians, Letter of Jeremiah, Preaching of Peter, Traditions of Matthias, Sibylline Oracles,* plus the Oral Gospel traditions not recorded.

Athanasius

Of particular importance in the selection of what became the Canon was Athanasius (296 –

373) who was the bishop of Alexandria. Each year he offered a Festal Letter that gave the date for the coming Easter. In his 39th such letter, he listed his selection for the canon. He listed the same twenty-seven books that comprise the New Testament today. But he also listed seven additional books that would not be accepted in the canon. Athanasius and his clergy would read aloud to their congregation from all of these texts.

The term 'apocrypha' was used by third century Egyptian Christians for those books attributable to such Old Testament figures as Moses and Enoch. Because these had been presumed lost after Rome expelled the Jews from Palestine, they caused quite a stir when they were later found. They were looked upon as special by third century Christians. Yet, of these additional books of the Old Testament, Athanasius calls most of them an invention of heretics.

In addition to apocrypha of the Old Testament, there were apocrypha for the New Testament as well. One of the most important of these was *The Shepherd.* It was composed in Rome while Pius was pope (140 – 154). Its author, Hermas, was Pius' brother! It reads as if

Hermas has had direct spiritual experience similar to those mentioned in the writings of John ("While I was in the spirit ..."[138]). It may have been excluded because of the esoteric rule that such knowledge ought not to be read to the uninitiated.

A remnant of a second century text called the Muratorian fragment is quoted here as it mentions Hermas as the author of *The Shepherd* and as the brother of Pius I and goes on to say, "And therefore it ought indeed to be read; but it cannot be read publicly to the people in church either among the Prophets, whose number is complete, or among the Apostles, for it is after their time." This quote offers remarkable insight into the feeling for the change away from the Mysteries and toward materialism in its times. The words still adhered to the notion that descriptions of the spiritual world were inappropriate for those unprepared.

Although Marcion compiled a list of acceptable books for his movement, the first canon similar to the modern one was this list found in the Muratorian fragment, compiled in 170. This list

---

[138] *Revelations* 1:10 and *The Shepherd of Hermas* 1:3

included all of the New Testament books except 1 Peter, 2 Peter, James, and 3 John and likely was available to Athanasius.

But the emerging Orthodox Church did not set its own canon until the fourth century. One of the tasks of the Council of Laodicea of 363 was to list and bless a canon of the New Testament. They also attempted to do so with the Old Testament. The council included 26 books for the New Testament but excluded Revelations. It included the current collection of the Old Testament books along with one book from the so-called Apocrypha. Then, in the reign of Theodosius I, the Council of Hippo in 393 added Revelations and the Council of Carthage in 397 affirmed these 27 books.

The first full "Bible" (Old and New Testaments) was completed in 405 by St. Jerome who selected books based on what he thought were authentic and spiritually inspired. His selection of 27 books aligned with those selected by the Council of Carthage. Note that over a hundred additional texts were considered but not selected.

When the word "Canon" is used, it typically means these 27 books. But the Church, in using Roman law as its model, sought to establish a *canon law* (from Greek kanon, a 'straight measuring rod') as a set of ecclesiastical ordinances and regulations to be used as its authority to enforce uniformity. We see the Church adopting Roman governance with canon law.

The following table shows 33 books that were considered for five different canons and which books were accepted and which were not for these various canons. Altogether, some 36 texts have been included in one canon or another, the list below shows the most common 33 texts that were accepted, rejected or merely consider.

	Book/Canon	Marcion	Muratoria	Peshitta	Alexandrinus	Modern
	Comment	Gnostic	Fragment list	Syriac	Greek Bible	Vulgate Bible
	Date	130 CE	170 CE	~180 CE	440 CE	4th C
1	Matthew	Yes	Yes	Yes	Yes	Yes
2	Mark	Yes	Yes	Yes	Yes	Yes
3	Luke	Yes	Yes	Yes	Yes	Yes
4	John	Yes	Yes	Yes	Yes	Yes
5	Acts	Yes	Yes	Yes	Yes	Yes
6	Romans	Yes	Yes	Yes	Yes	Yes
7	1 Corinthians	Yes	Yes	Yes	Yes	Yes
8	2 Corinthians	Yes	Yes	Yes	Yes	Yes
9	Galatians	Yes	Yes	Yes	Yes	Yes
10	Ephesians	Yes	Yes	Yes	Yes	Yes
11	Philippians	Yes	Yes	Yes	Yes	Yes
12	Colossians	Yes	Yes	Yes	Yes	Yes
13	1 Thessalonians	Yes	Yes	Yes	Yes	Yes
14	2 Thessalonians	Yes	Yes	Yes	Yes	Yes
15	1 Timothy	Yes	Yes	Yes	Yes	Yes
16	2 Timothy	Yes	Yes	Yes	Yes	Yes
17	Titus	Yes	Yes	Yes	Yes	Yes
18	Philemon	Yes	Yes	Yes	Yes	Yes
19	Hebrews	Yes	Yes	Yes	Yes	Yes
20	James	No	No	Yes	Yes	Yes
21	1 Peter	No	No	Yes	Yes	Yes
22	2 Peter	No	No	No	Yes	Yes
23	1 John	Yes	Yes	Yes	Yes	Yes
24	2 John	Yes	Yes	No	Yes	Yes
25	3 John	Maybe	Maybe	No	Yes	Yes
26	Jude	Yes	Yes	No	Yes	Yes
27	Revelations	Yes	Yes	No	Yes	Yes
28	Apoclypse Peter	Yes	Yes	No	No	No
29	Solomon	Yes	Yes	No	No	No
30	1 Clement	No	No	No	Yes	No
31	2 Clement	No	No	No	Yes	No
32	Hermas	No	No	No	No	No
33	Barnabas	No	No	No	No	No

7. Theological Debates of Early Christianity

Because all of the disciples plus Paul were raised as Jews with Jewish customs, there was great difficulty separating from these Jewish roots. Traditions, laws, and theologies had deep roots. Paul led the movement to expand beyond its Jewish base. Outside this monotheistic base, Christianity encountered pagan polytheism and the dying ancient Mysteries.

As new members converted from their old beliefs and practices to Christianity, one of the first theological issues to be met was the concept of the Trinity. Luckily, as we discussed, this concept had already been developed during the Egyptian-Chaldean-Babylonian era (roughly 3000 to 800 BCE). In addition, questions about the entelechy of Jesus and Christ raged. Were they a combined entity with Christ the divine part and Jesus the human being? Were they two halves joined together? One view that emerged was that He was "a unity of both divine and human" (the Hypostatic union) as opposed to both Adoptionism (that Jesus was only human) and Docetism (that Christ was only divine). Was

Christ both invisible and visible? Imponderable and ponderable? Incapable and capable of suffering? Inexpressible and expressible in writing? Could and should the new Christianity express itself out of the existing Hellenistic philosophies?

Lastly, what should Christianity do with the Old Testament? Was it needed for the new religion? If Christianity was to cast off the ancient Mysteries, should it not cast off its Jewish roots too? Did Christ's new covenant supersede the Mosaic covenant?

In his five books against Marcion, Tertullian proclaimed the emerging Orthodox theology as opposed to any Hellenistic streams. He had learned the Greek philosophies but rejected them. Where Origen of Alexandria aligned his story of Creation with Platonism, Tertullian carried his realism deeper into materialism. We see this first when he ascribed corporeity to God but even more so with his acceptance of the Traducian theory of the origin of the soul.[139] He comes to the conclusion that Plato,

---

[139] Traducian, which comes from 'branch of a vine' means "that every human being is a 'branch' off of his or her parents. Both soul and body are generated by father and mother. This is in opposition to the creationist view that says God creates every new soul" directly at

Aristotle, and other Greek thinkers were the patriarchal forefathers of the heretics (*De anima*, III.). In the post-Nicene period in the West, his writings eventually took on a formative influence upon western theology. But, with a romantic memory of the Mysteries and the great Philosophers still lingering, no theologian during the third century referenced his works. Theologians were stuck between the glorious past and a dark, materialistic future until Augustine, in the fifth century, was able to resolve this by adding Faith to the existing role of Knowledge into the emerging theology and by giving Tertullian high respect.

From Oral to Written to Adulteration to Canon

The Center for the Study of New Testament Manuscripts reports in their blog[140] that they have a manuscript (GA 2907) that contains different words that those that appear today in the four Gospels and other books. The blog shows photographs that reveal the alteration by a later scribe of the original. Likely this was

---

conception, or at implantation, or at birth. See https://www.str.org/blog/how-did-you-get-a-soul-creationism-versus-traducianism

[140] http://csntm.org/Resources/Blog, accessed 4Sep2019

done in order to change the meaning of the end of Matthew 2 and the beginning of Matthew 3. The blog also points out a change in the normal title *The Gospel According to Mark.* In their GA 2907 manuscript, the title of the text reads *The Gospel* ***from*** *'According to Mark'!* This helps to confirm our earlier discussion that *Secret Mark* was the basis for Mark's gospel. Lastly, the blog mentions that the original scribe does not include John 7:52 to 8:12.[141] This suggests that either

- the original John did not have this passage and it was added not by the original author or
- this scribe did not want to include it for some reason.

In Galatians 3:28, Paul stressed what was new with Christianity, that "there is no longer Jew or Greek, there is no longer slave or free, there is no longer male and female; for all of you are one in Christ Jesus."[142] In Romans 16, Paul offered a number of greetings to women and speaks of the church role of Phoebe. In all of the letters of the New Testament, she is the

---

[141] IBID accessed 7July2018

[142] Galatians 3:28, NIV

only person to have been so commended by Paul.

So how could Paul also write "Let a woman learn in silence in all submissiveness. I permit no woman to teach or have authority over men; she is to keep silent"?[143] Or "As in all the congregations of the Lord's people, women should remain silent in the churches. They are not allowed to speak, but must be in submission, *as the law says*. If they want to inquire about something, they should ask their own husbands at home; for it is disgraceful for a woman to speak in the church."[144]

Many theological historians such as Barbara Leonhard, Bart Ehrman, Jerome Murphy-O'Connor, Evelyn and Frank Stagg, and John Wijngaards all believe this to be a "post-Pauline interpolation" or an outright adulteration of the letter in order to maintain the old laws.[145]

---

[143] 1 Tim. 2:11, NIV

[144] 1 Corinthians 14:33-35, NIV

[145] Barbara Leonhard, "St. Paul and Women: A Mixed Record", *St. Anthony Messenger*, Franciscan Media. Jerome Murphy-O'Connor, *Paul: His Story*, Oxford University Press, 2006. Bart Ehrman, *Peter, Paul, and Mary Magdalene: The Followers of Jesus in History and Legend*, Oxford University Press, 2006. Evelyn and Frank

In his letter to the Ephesians, the Apostle Paul cited from Genesis 2:24 "That is why a man will leave his father and mother and be united to his wife, and the two will become one flesh. This is a profound mystery."[146] What makes it so profound or a mystery? Because of its truth on multiple levels! And because it speaks of the two that become one. Christian Egalitarian theologians have found this concept of the "two becoming one" significant for the role of women in marriage and in the Church. They also point to the teachings of Christ-Jesus regarding marriage in Matthew and Mark, "and the two will become one flesh. So, they are no longer two, but one flesh. Therefore, what God has joined together, let no one separate."[147] Could this point to a future mystical marriage within oneself that overcomes gender delineations? Early Greek mythology suggests that there was a time when the gods and humans were hermaphrodites. Does such a destiny await humanity? Materialism scoffs at such a notion.

Stagg, *Woman in the World of Jesus*, Westminster, 1978. J. Wijngaards. *No Women in Holy Orders? The Women Deacons of the Early Church,* 2002

[146] Ephesians 5:31-32

[147] Matthew 19:5-6 and Mark 10:8-9

Christianity After Gnosticism

After Gnosticism was exiled to history, Christian theology in the fourth century could safely set its theological sights on the physical world as the creation and manifestation of God. And it could focus on Christ as the one and only God. As these two pillars of theology emerged, the theology of a heavenly hierarchy of beings faded away. Three centuries later, when the message of Islam "there is only one God: Allah, and Muhammed was his prophet" came into conflict with Christianity, Christians countered with the message that "there is only one God (that we need to be concerned with), and that God is Christ." After the seventh century, many materialistic similarities in theology were expressed in both Christianity and Islam. Was this an expression of a theological truth or the underlying philosophy that pervaded the times, i.e., materialism?

The Christianity that won the Heresy Wars had its roots in the Christianity brought to the West by John, son of Zebedee. But its first heresy warrior, Irenaeus, likely would not have recognized the Christianity that emerged from the fourth to the seventh century when imperial directives were issued with the intention of homogenizing the nascent religion.

Multiple decrees had been issued by Theodosius I between 381 to 391. The first sought to excommunicate any and all non-conformists. Each round became more severe until the later decrees sought to exterminate, to root out and destroy any and all (especially Christians) who would not declare their strict allegiance to the new and evolving Nicene creed.

With troops mandated to enforce these decrees, mobs took matters into their hands too. The great sage, Hypatia of Alexandria was brutally dismembered alive by a mob in 415 because of her Neoplatonist beliefs that had now been labeled heretical. Some Early Christians had anticipated an End of the World would arrive in their lifetime. As for the Mysteries and for spiritual knowledge, their world did end by the close of the fourth century.

As mentioned, later Byzantine emperors complete this annihilation. Justinian, in seeking to restore the Roman Empire to its former glory, sought unity not only in government but also in religion. He wanted a single, universal set of beliefs. He sought this goal through imperial might. Naturally, this led to the growth of dogma out of a faith that had been kidnapped by materialism. Justinian closed all mystery schools including the Dionysian Platonic Academy, the School of Athens that had been established by St. Paul. His soldiers and mobs went further to actually tear down some of the remaining oracles and mystery centers.

It became the time for the Rule of Faith.

From Excommunication to Extermination

What St. Paul was to the Hellenistic West, Mani or Manes (216 – 276) was to the Buddhist and Zoroastrian East. Like Paul, Mani had significant spiritual revelations. The first was at age twelve and the second was at age twenty-four.[148] More may have followed according to a twelve-year rhythm, but these were not recorded.

---

[148] The alignment of Mani's age for his first spiritual event with the event in the Temple of Jerusalem for Jesus in Luke is noteworthy.

Mani built a Christian Church peacefully within the Persian empire. He converted many of Persia's royalty. Once established, Manichaeism spread with extraordinary speed not only in the east, but also in the west. In 244 CE, it was established in Egypt. Mani's apostle Psattiq, like St. Peter, brought this branch of Christianity to Rome in 280 CE. By 312 CE, several Manichaean monasteries operated in Rome. Its rapid spread showed that its spiritual basis aligned with the evolving spiritual mood of its time.

Persecution of the Manichaeans

For the Orthodox Church, no heretic received from them more derision and brutal opposition than did Mani. Not only was the emerging Catholicism threatened but the long-established Persian religion Zoroastrianism was as well. Mani and his expanding followers soon found themselves subject to vicious persecution ironically similar to that suffered by the early Christians at the hands of the Roman empire. Wherever Manichaeism spread, persecution followed. In 291 under Persian Emperor Bahram II, many Manichaeans were slaughtered including their leading apostle Sisin. In the Roman Empire, Diocletian decreed in 296: "We order that their

[Manichaean] organizers and leaders be subject to the final penalties and condemned to the fire with their abominable scriptures." The status of martyrdom resulted for most living in the Eastern Roman Empire. Hilary of Poitiers wrote in 354, that those of the Manichaean faith were a significant portion of the population of southern Gaul (today France). In the years following 381, they disappear in southern Gaul after Theodosius I, under pressure from Christian theologians, removed their civil rights. Further edicts by Theodosius I in 382 sought to fully uproot Manichaeism so it would never grow back. Even sympathizers were punished. Oddly, nearly a thousand years later, history in this region would repeat itself with the Albigensian Crusade and the Inquisition. More on those later in this book.

One of the most significant Church leaders of this period, St. Augustine, had been a Manichaean for nearly ten years. But in 387, notably at the age of 33, Augustine of Hippo (354–430) converted to Christianity. This was just as the Decree of Death for all Manichaean monks had been issued by Theodosius I and implementation had begun. Yet another anti-Manichaean-inspired decree by Theodosius I, in 391, declared Christianity to be the only legitimate religion for the Roman Empire. Perhaps Augustine's words, "I would not believe the gospel were it not that the authority of the Catholic Church compels me to do so"[149] were in response.

With this deadly persecution, the religion was essentially removed from Western Europe before the sixth century. It lingered longer in the Eastern Roman Empire but disappeared before the end of the sixth century. It survived much longer within those states where Islam had become the state religion as Manichaeism was tolerated by the Muslim states. However, Manichaeans within the Islamic caliphates were taxed heavily and treated poorly for a century, until, in 780, Harun al-Rashid of Baghdad restored tolerance of this religion. In CE 1000, although exterminated in the West, the Arab historian Al-Beruni wrote: "The majority of the Eastern Turks, the inhabitants of China and Tibet, and a number in India belong to the religion of Mani." How these remaining Manichaean communities died out is not known but following the Crusades and

[149] *The Confessions of St. Augustine*, translated by F. J. Sheed, Sheed and Ward, 1944

the brutal Christian-Mongol Invasions, Manichaeism did fade away in each of these remaining areas.

Confluence of Mystic Streams into Manichaeism

Augustine's *Confessions* described his time as a Manichaean "hearer"[150] as well as his partially successful attempt at a Manichaean initiation. Once Augustine became an Orthodox Christian, he became an adversary of Manichaeism. In fairness, he wrote, "Though Mani called himself the Paraclete, he claimed no divinity. But, with a show of humility, he styled himself an "Apostle of Jesus Christ by the providence of God the Father." Such a claim would mean that the Word of God had not ceased its flow with Paul but could continue with others! Over 1500 years later, the Mormon Church would make a similar claim that inspired words can still flow from the heavenly realm.

[150] Manichaeism members could be a "hearer" or those who came to church but had not made a Christian vow, the "elect" were those who had committed themselves to a Christian life via an oath, and higher levels of commitment for "presbyters" and "bishops" and "apostles" and Patriarch or "Father".

With the extermination of Manichaeism and its texts in the western world, the Roman Church could focus its attention on non-Gnostic heresies: Arianism and Nestorianism. But Manichaeism persisted outside the Roman Empire and new Manichaean communities would pop up from time to time. The Paulicians, Bogomils, and Cathars apparently had roots in Manichaeism.

There are two different accounts of Mani's childhood. One claims Mani's parents had belonged to the Gnostic-Christian (and Jewish) sect called the Elcesaites. This branch of Christianity was greatly influenced by Gnosticism and the attainment of spiritual union through knowledge and inner development. The ancient philosophies of Empedocles and Pythagoras were taught to Mani. The other comes from historian Socrates Scholasticus who wrote,

"A Saracen named Scythian married a captive from the Upper Thebes. On her account he dwelt in Egypt and having versed himself in the learning of the Egyptians, he subtly introduced the theory of Empedocles and Pythagoras among the doctrines of the Christian faith. Asserting that there were two natures, a good

and an evil one, he termed, as Empedocles had done, the latter Discord, and the former Friendship. Of this Scythian, Buddas, who had been previously called Terebinthus, became a disciple; and he, having proceeded to Babylon, which the Persians inhabit, made many extravagant statements respecting himself, declaring that he was born of a virgin, and brought up in the mountains. The same man afterwards composed four books, one he entitled The Mysteries, *another* The Gospel, *a third* The Treasure, *and the fourth* Heads [Summaries]*; but pretending to perform some mystic rites, he was hurled down a precipice by a spirit, and so perished. A certain woman at whose house he had lodged buried him, and taking possession of his property, bought a boy about seven years old whose name was Cubricus: this lad she enfranchised, and having given him a liberal education, she soon after died, leaving him all that belonged to Terebinthus, including the books he had written on the principles inculcated by Scythian. Cubricus, the freedman, taking these things with him and having withdrawn into the regions of Persia, changed his name, calling himself Manes; and disseminated the books of Buddas or Terebinthus among his deluded* *followers as his own. Now the contents of these treatises apparently agree with Christianity in expression but are pagan in sentiment: for Manichæus being an atheist, incited his disciples to acknowledge a plurality of gods, and taught them to worship the sun. He also introduced the doctrine of Fate, denying human free-will; and affirmed a transmutation of bodies, clearly following the opinions of Empedocles, Pythagoras, and the Egyptians. He denied that Christ existed in the flesh, asserting that he was an apparition; and rejected moreover the law and the prophets, calling himself the 'Comforter,'—all of which dogmas are totally at variance with the orthodox faith of the church."*[151]

Legend claims that the great teacher Scythianus,[152] taught Mani, either directly or indirectly. Scythianus taught him that all the ancient Mysteries and religions pointed

---

151 https://www.ccel.org/ccel/schaff/npnf202.ii.iv.xxii.html accessed 18Aug2018

152 Scythianus was a significant teacher of Alexandria. He visited India around 50 CE. He is mentioned by several Christian writers including Hippolytus who wrote that he brought "the doctrine of the Two Principles" from India and later he became Mani's teacher. These Two Principles describe polarities.

towards the coming of Christianity. It is, therefore, not surprising that one finds elements of Buddhism, Zorastrianism, Empedocles, and Pythagoras in Mani's own teachings as each of these, in this view, were part of the process leading towards the coming of the Christ Event. Augustine would take a view similar[153] to Mani's view that the prior religions and the ancient mysteries anticipated the coming of the Cosmic Christ. One of earliest of the Church Fathers, Clement of Alexandria (150 – 215) also held a view that the Christ already existed in the spiritual realms before the Baptism. Similar to how Paul spoke to leaders of the various Hellenistic Mystery Centers, Mani would attempt to show to a local religion that what they were expecting was indeed the Christ; and that He had come. Like Paul, Mani used the local sacred texts or traditions to prove this.

---

[153] St. Augustine also wrote, "What is now called the Christian religion already existed among the ancients and was not lacking at the very beginnings of the human race. When Christ appeared in the flesh, the true religion already in existence received the name of Christian." *Retractions* Book I, chapter 12, section 3, from *The Fathers of the Church* trans. Mary Inez Bogan, Catholic University of America Press, 1968.

Manichaean Theology: Reincarnation and Overcoming Evil

Largely because Mani's theology was woven with knowledge of reincarnation and karma; it became anathema to the Roman Church. To Mani, Christ' Resurrection had solved the question of death but from now on the Christian focus was to be on another problem, overcoming evil. For Mani, Christ's Resurrection was the turning point in a human evolution. A new way to the spirit was opened for each individual to tread. But it required each individual to act, to walk the path on his or her own, to carry his or her cross. This may require multiple lifetimes to perfect the soul. And perfection did not mean a reward of eternal rest in cosmic bliss, but rather an enablement to then help towards the perfection of all of humanity.

As such, Mani's theology dealt with the Christian relationship to evil. Evil was to be overcome as a final goal of a human evolution. For such an outcome, reincarnation played a vital role. This may be understood best by a Manichaean story, the Legend of Light and Dark: Creation had begun out of the fire of Divine Love. Later, from this fire both lightness and darkness were created. After some time, the Dark became imbued with greed and thus sought to enter Light's domain.[154] *Original Mankind* was sent to meet the forces of Darkness. Where the Dark met the Light, a kind of vortex formed. Into this *Original Mankind* fell. Also, from the Dark, Death fell into the vortex too. Thus, Mankind became a mix of Light and Dark, of Good and Evil. In addition, Death became a part of the experience of Man in the vortex. [This story shares many themes with the Fall of Man from Genesis. This *Original Man* compares to *Adam Kadmon* who, in Kabbalistic terminology was what was held back of the archetype of Mankind.

In Mani's theology, Fallen Man is to be rescued. To create the "landing spot" for the Fall, the Divine Forces worked with the Demiurge[155] to forge a new creation between light and dark. For the redemption of Fallen Man, the physical world had to come into being out of the prior one. This required the creative work of the Demiurge. From the Divine, the Calling (the Word), begins to sound.

---

[154] In some esoteric traditions this is called the War in Heaven.

[155] It is not clear to which forces the Demiurge belonged (light or dark).

The Calling is to the inner being, to what in Fallen Man is from above, namely Life within Mankind.[156] This Calling is what would eventually descend "as a dove"[157] upon the body of Jesus at his baptism to become Jesus-Christ. This new creation, i.e. the physical world, came into being from the prior one through the work of spiritual beings who were lower in the hierarchy than the original creative beings.

In Manichaeism, Christ is the Calling, the Word, the Logos. His Calling was not to the physical as it was believed that the physical will pass away. Rather the Calling sounded above the physical in what is Life within Mankind (and thus will not pass away).

Next can come the Answer. It comes from each human being who, through his or her own effort, becomes the tenth hierarchy [Manichaeism also spoke of nine levels above Mankind]. Following this, yet a new creation out of the recovered light, out of what Mankind has gained can come into being [this relates the parable of talents where three sons

---

[156] Life was envisioned as a higher state than the physical and from the Kingdom of Light.
[157] Matthew 3:16

are given talents. One hides it in order to return it all as it was given. And the other two have risked their talents to bring back more than the original.][158] In this way, Mankind, becomes the tenth hierarchy, and then participates in a future third creation.[159]

Later Resurrections of Manichaeism

Although Manichaeans were slaughtered as heretics throughout the Roman empires leading to their extermination by the end of the sixth century, several later groups seem to be linked to them. The practices and theologies of the Paulicians, the Bogomils, and

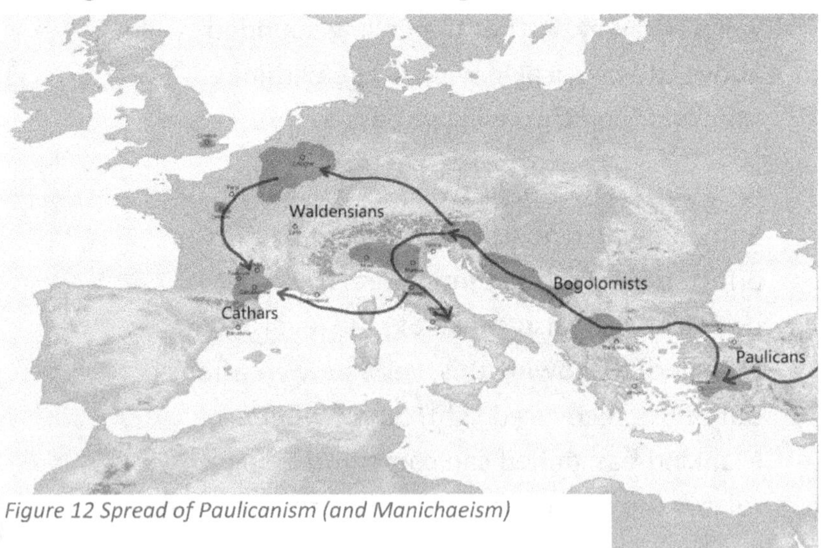

Figure 12 Spread of Paulicanism (and Manichaeism)

---

[158] Matthew 25:14-30

[159] In Esoteric lore, this creation is called Jupiter (and has nothing to do with the physical planet called Jupiter)

then the Cathars all carry such remarkable similarities to Manichaeism that one could easily conclude that these were offspring of Manichaeism. Or, perhaps some Manichaeans came as missionaries from distant lands to found these communities.

Paulicianism becomes labeled by the Catholic Church a heresy in the mid-seventh century. Their founder, Constantine of Mananalis, had taught about both a good God who had made the souls of humans, and a lesser (perhaps evil) God who had created everything physical in the universe including the human body. Constantine of Mananalis was able to base his teachings entirely upon the New Testament! But, under pressure from the Church, Byzantine emperor John I Tzimiskes (mercifully) forced the entire population of Armenian Paulicians to migrate to Thrace in 970. History lists this exodus at about 200,000. Here they become known as the Bogomils. They lived in harmony with the Bulgarians until 1650 when the Roman Catholic Church forced them to convert or die.

With Cathar communities within Florence and nearby, Renaissance artists such as Leonardo da Vinci were aware of their beliefs and their positive effects on the social and economic life of their region. And he likely knew of the Albigensian Crusade and the slaughter of these non-violent Christians who had ties to Manichaeism. [For more on the Cathars see page 227].

Heretics Aplenty

Arising out of multiple Christianities, Early Christianity was awash with so-called heretics. To round out this topic, here are some of the other well-known heretics.

Marcion

Marcion influenced Christian theology from the second to the sixth century.

Like the Gnostics, Marcionism was an Early Christian dualist belief system. Marcion (85-160) affirmed Christ was the savior sent by God and Paul was his chief apostle. But he saw a clear difference between the Father God Christ prayed to and the Father God of the Jews. According to Marcion, the Demiurge who created the material universe was the Father God of the Old Testament. This god was a jealous tribal deity of the Jews who asked his people to follow the rule “an eye for an eye.” This god punishes for one’s sins through suffering and death. The Father God of Christ was a God of who looked upon humanity with benevolence and mercy. Marcion of Sinope attracted large followings to his teachings in Rome around the year 144. Many early apologists, such as Tertullian on his Adversus Marcionem (year 207) condemned Marcionism. Marcionism continued in the West for 300 years, although Marcionistic ideas persisted much longer. Marcionism continued in the East for some centuries further.

Montanus

Montanus influenced Christian theology from the late second to the fourth century.

Montanus preached that the workings of the Holy Spirit at Pentecost can continue for those properly prepared. Miraculous gifts and spiritual inspirations, even prophecy, did not cease with the disciples. He claimed that each person was capable of inner transformation to become a vehicle for the Paraclete (Holy Spirit). Christ had promised this. His opponents claim his pride led him to teach that individuals such as himself could rise spiritually above even that of the Church. One of the derogatory falsely claims against him is that he thought Christ would soon return and come to his hometown in Phrygia.

Sabellius

Sabellius influenced Christian theology from the early third to the fourth century.

The Sabellianists taught that the Father, Son, and Holy Spirit are three different aspects of the One, the Godhead. The Trinity exists only in mankind's ponderable perspective of God's imponderable reality. Orthodoxy's Trinitarianism saw three distinct beings within the Godhead.

Arius

Arius influenced Christian theology from the fourth to the ninth century.

The Council of Nicaea dealt with the theology of Arius (256 – 336) who, in wrestling with the concepts of a one God or of a Trinity, opposed the new philosophy of the fourth century from Athanasius of Alexandria that proclaimed that the Son is of one nature, of the same substance (homoousios) as the Father God.

Arius felt that each member of the Trinity was of a different substance (heteroousia). In this debate over the *substance* of spiritual beings, we see the penetration of materialism into theology. Arians felt the Son was indeed from the Father but not the same as the Father and especially not of the same substance as that of the Father. They cite Christ's prayers to the Father and to the Gospel's implication that it was the Father who raised the Christ on Easter

Figure 13 Arian Baptistry, sixth century mosaic, Ravenna

morning as proof that the Son God was subordinate to the Father God. Arians, in their theology, allowed for multiple gods in a hierarchy whose members were subordinate to the one God, the Father. We see the depiction of lesser gods in their fifth century baptistry in Ravenna where at the baptism of Jesus, the god of the River Jordan is portrayed. Such iconography never existed in the sanctioned art of the Roman Church.

Emperor Constantius was an avowed Arian. He became sole Roman ruler in 350. At this point, Christianity could have adopted Arianism if not for the tenacious adherence to Orthodoxy by Athanasius. He wrote to his Church in Alexandria in his Festal Letter 29, while he was in exile, "I know moreover that not only this thing saddens you, but also the fact that while others have obtained the churches by violence, you are meanwhile cast out from your places. For they [the Arians] hold the places, but you the Apostolic Faith. They are, it is true, in the places, but outside of the true Faith; while you are outside the places indeed, but the Faith, within you. Let us consider whether is the greater, the place or the Faith. Clearly the true Faith. Who then has lost more, or who possesses more? He who holds the place, or he who holds the Faith?"

In his book, *Manual of Church History,* Professor Thomas Gilmartin describes the drama that almost brought Arianism to rule the Church, "The Arians sought the approval of an Ecumenical Council. They sought to hold two councils. Constantius, summoned the bishops of the East to meet at Seleucia in Isauria, and those of the West to Rimini in Italy. A preliminary conference was held by the Arians at Sirmium, to agree a formula of faith. A 'Homoeon' creed was adopted, declaring The Son to be 'like the Father'. The two [councils] met in autumn of 359. At Seleucia, one hundred and fifty bishops, of which one hundred and five were semi-Arian. The semi-Arians refused to accept anything less than the 'Homoiousion' formulary of faith [a compromise between homoousios and heteroousia]. The Imperial Prefect was obliged to disband, without agreeing on any creed."[160] At Rimini the orthodox greatly outnumbered the Arian delegates but again no agreement on a creed change could be reached. Constantius,

[160] Thomas Gilmartin, Manual of Church History, Vol. 1, Chapter 17, St. Patrick's College, 1926

using his imperial powers, prevailed on them to accept the Sirmian creed. It was after this Council that Jerome said: "... the whole world groaned in astonishment to find itself Arian."

But Emperor Constantius died on 4 November 361. Theological chaos emerged as the next emperor, Julian the Apostate, could not understand why the glorious ancient Mysteries had been abandoned for what he saw as a much lesser religion, Christianity. While Julian sought to restore these Mysteries to their former glory, mobs of pagan supporters murdered the Arian bishop of Alexandria. Coincidentally, Julian issued a religious-tolerance edict that permitted all exiled bishops to return to their provinces. Thus, Athanasius returned to Alexandria in 362. There he reinforced the orthodox doctrine of the Trinity.

Julian, in his attempt to restore the Mysteries, senses that Athanasius is becoming too strong so he sends him into exile into Upper Egypt. A year later, Julian was murdered by his own Christian soldiers in Persia. When word of this arrived, Athanasius returned in secret to Alexandria. The new emperor, Jovian, restored Christianity to its place as the state religion and he also restored Athanasius to his former position.

Jovian's rule, however, was short lived. The next two Arian-leaning emperors also shortly succumbed to death. And in 366 Pope Liberius died. He was succeeded by Pope Damasus who decreed that no Bishop should be consecrated unless he held the Creed of Nicea.[161] After five exiles, Athanasius is finally able to return to Alexandria in 366 for his last seven years of life. There he consolidates Orthodoxy and the Nicene doctrine of homoousios.

Although Arius (250 – 336) was declared to be a heretic in 381, his bishop, Ulfilas, had already begun to convert the Gothic tribes to Arian Christianity. These former barbarians later overran much of the western Roman Empire including the sacking of Rome by King Alaric and his Visigoths in 410. Hence, the power of Catholicism would reside in the eastern Roman empire until the time of Pepin (714 – 768) and Charlemagne (742 – 814) when deceit would return power to the Roman Catholic Church.[162]

---

[161] F. A. Forbes, *Saint Athanasius*, R&T Washbourne, 1919

[162] The Donation of Constantine was a forged document.

Pelagius (influence from fifth – eighth century)

Pelagius influenced Christian theology from the fifth to the eighth century.

Pelagius, from Ireland, battles with Augustine for the soul of Christianity. He denied that we inherit original sin from the Fall. Rather, each human was created sinless but through life acquired sin. He said that by elevating evil to the same status as God and by teaching pagan fatalism, Augustine was still under the influence of Manichaeism. Likewise, Pelagius denied that we automatically inherit righteousness as a result of Christ's death on Golgotha. Rather, Pelagius stated that man is born morally neutral and can achieve righteousness under the powers granted each individual by Christ. These powers exist in one's own free will. Pelagius placed the onus on each person's own inner life. Prayer, fasting, and asceticism helped educate and strengthen the will to do the good. However, Augustine's view that people cannot come to God without the grace of God was adopted by the Church and Pelagius was excommunicated in 418 and forced to live in an Egyptian oasis under Cyril of Alexandria's watch. While there, he disappears and never found. In 431, with Pelagius' supporters either excommunicated or dead, Augustine managed to get him declared to be a heretic by the First Council of Ephesus. However, his views on free will lived on especially in Britain where they came to greatly influence western thought.

Nestorius

Nestorius influenced Christian theology from the fifth to the fourteenth century.

Nestorius (386 – 450) originated from the Christian center at Antioch and became the bishop of Constantinople for 3.5 years until condemned by Theodosius II in 431 and confirmed later that year by the Council of Ephesus. He had denied that Mary had given birth to a divine being. Rather, he claimed, Jesus was a man. Thus, the title of Theotokos (Greek: "God-bearer" or, less literally, "Mother of God") was incorrect. This debate had similarities to the proto-Orthodox debates with the Gnostics. Nestorius pointed to the baptism as when Christ entered human nature.

Christ was not in her womb. As a compromise, he proposed giving Mary the alternative title Christotokos ("Christ-bearer" or "Mother of Christ").

Where Arius had questioned the *substance* of each member of the Trinity, Nestorius questioned the *composition* of Christianity's most important individual, Christ-Jesus. Nestorians felt that Mary gave birth to a *human* Jesus naturally, even if as a virgin. The fifth century concept of *Theotokos*, the Bearer of God (or the Mother of God) reduced the Baptism to an act of anointing. Nestorians would elaborate by saying that Jesus grew up as a man, not as a divine being; that is until his baptism when, at age 30, he was united with the divine spirit of the Christ. After the baptism, the composition of this individual then became body (*soma*) from Jesus and spirit (*pneuma*) from Christ replacing the spirit of the man Jesus. The middle entity, soul (*psyche*), would have needed to be highly developed one prior to the baptism so that during the coming three years the Christ spirit that inhabited this composition, could quickly penetrate and transform first this soul and later the body. Preparation of a body able to bear the Christ within, would be another mystery beyond the scope of this book.[163] The Christ-transformed soul was revealed at the Transfiguration followed by the transformed body at Easter (or just before the crucifixion when Christ-Jesus proclaims, "The hour has come that Son of Man should be glorified)."[164]

Orthodox Catholic theologians reasoned that Nestorius's theology must divide Jesus-Christ into two separate entities, one human and one divine. Such a concept was losing to the potent strength of materialism arising in the fifth century. In 431 the Council of Ephesus was convened to deal with Nestorianism. It granted Mary the title of Mother of God, that the person she carried in her womb was, in fact, God incarnate ("in the flesh"). At this point, the significance of the baptism was lost.

Not until this century did the Assyrian Church of the East, historically regarded as the last remnant of the Nestorian church, sign a fully orthodox joint declaration on Christology with the Catholic Church that rejected

---

[163] See *The Hidden Heretic of the Renaissance: Leonardo* by this author, Andrew Linnell
[164] John 12:23

Nestorianism. Materialism had conquered Nestorianism.

What took place at the Council of Ephesus was a tragedy for Christianity. When Nestorius' rival, Cyril of Alexandria, heard that the boat carrying the sympathizers of Nestorius was delayed, he quickly convened the Council and immediately called for a vote to condemn Nestorius. Before the council closed its agenda, John I of Antioch and the eastern bishops arrived. They were furious to hear that Nestorius had already been condemned. Thus, they convened their own synod to depose Cyril for un-Christian behavior. Both sides then appealed to the emperor.

Following political correctness, Theodosius ordered both Nestorius and Cyril to be deposed and exiled. Nestorius was made to return to his monastery at Antioch, and Maximian was consecrated Archbishop of Constantinople in his place. Cyril was soon allowed to return to his post after bribing various courtiers. In the following months, he successfully removed 17 of the bishops who had supported Nestorius's doctrine and replaced them with his supporters. Outflanked, John I of Antioch was forced to abandon Nestorius in 433 or lose his position.

On August 3, 435 CE, Nestorius was exiled, like Pelagius, to an oasis in Egypt by an edict from Theodosius II. Cyril had won through brutality. The issue of the Birth would not surface again (although Leonardo da Vinci seems to have known about this when he painted the *Virgin of the Rocks)*.[165]

The devoted followers of Nestorius then split off and founded the Christian Church of the Orient that became, by the end of the first Millennium, the largest Christian church spreading through Persia, India, Kazakhstan, China, and had outposts as far away as Japan.

Monophysitism

Monophysitism influenced Christian theology during the fifth century.

Monophysitism originated as a reaction to Nestorianism. The Monophysites (led by a man named Eutyches) were horrified by Nestorius's implication that Christ was two people with

---

[165] Again,see *The Hidden Heretic of the Renaissance: Leonardo* by this author, Andrew Linnell

two different natures (human and divine). They went to the other extreme, claiming that Christ was one person with only one nature (a fusion of human and divine elements). They are thus known as Monophysites because of their claim that Christ had only one nature (Greek: mono = one; physis = nature).

Orthodox Catholic theologians recognized that Monophysitism was as bad as Nestorianism because it denied Christ's full humanity and his full divinity. If Christ did not have a fully human nature, then he would not be fully human, and if he did not have a fully divine nature then he was not fully divine.

Iconoclasm

Iconoclasm was a response to the devotion of icons that influenced Christian theology during the seventh and eighth centuries.

In Islam, it was forbidden to have religious images. Their art was relegated to beautiful geometric and foliage patterns. The question arose then in Christianity if it was permissible to depict the divine. The Ten Commandments forbade the making and worshipping of "graven images."[166] A group known as iconoclasts (literally, "icon smashers") grew into a movement that eventually convinced Emperor Leo III to ban icons. They claimed it was sinful to venerate pictures and statues of Christ or the saints. The icon-battles were fought in 726 to 787 and again 814 to 842 mostly in the Byzantine regions. Empress Theodora (815 – 868?), a lover of Icons, prevailed and restored icon veneration while convincing the Church to declare the iconoclasts as heretics.

Why were there so many heretics? Starting with twelve Christianities, it was natural that there would be different beliefs. Add to this the lingering initiates from the ancient Mysteries and some new Christian initiates from the secret Christian groups that were still training students. Thus, multiple beliefs were bound to appear. With the rise of individual intellectualism, egoism and group egoism crept in. Today some of these theological battles seem petty, even silly.

---

[166] see Exodus 20:4

8. The East-West Split of Christianity

As we have seen, in 325 when Constantine ordered the First Ecumenical Council to convene, he wanted the theological bickering to stop. He hoped to bring the multiple Christianities into one, universal and uniform theology. The term Catholic, meaning universal, derives from this intention.

Thereafter, materialism flexed its muscles through imperial military might. Fifty-five years later, Theodosius I would issue a series of decrees that rendered Nicene Christianity, as the official state church of the Roman Empire. From that point on, until the Reformation, there was but one Christianity of the Roman Empire with all the other Christianities and all other religions forced underground.

These edicts aided mobs in their gleeful destruction of the mystery centers including prominent Hellenistic temples such as the Temple of Apollo in Delphi and the Serapeum in Alexandria. Theodosius I tried to separate the new Christianity from the past by dissolving all pagan remnants such as the Order of the Vestal Virgins in Rome and the pagan rituals performed at the Olympics in

Greece. After his death, Theodosius' young sons Arcadius and Honorius each inherited a half of the Empire. Never again would the Roman Empire be re-united as a state.

The East-West split deepened at the end of the ninth century when two Councils of Constantinople were held ten years apart. In the first, the West condemned the East. In the second, the East condemned the West. Father Francis Dvornik[167] and Cardinal Yves Congar[168] detailed in their books how Pope John VIII ratified the acts of the second of these Councils of Constantinople. The first was held in 869 while the second was held in 879. By ratifying the second council, the Pope made it law and ecumenical in both the West and East. The Pope and his legates signed off on four principles:

1. That the Nicene Creed would be restored to its original form (minus the Filioque that will be discussed later
2. That Photius was indeed the legitimate Patriarch of Constantinople

---

[167] Francis Dvornik, *The Ecumenical Councils,* Twentieth Century Encyclopedia of Catholicism 82. Hawthorn Books, 1961

[168] Yves Congar, *True and False Reform in the Church*, Transl. Paul Philibert, Glazier, 2010

3. That the Pope, as Patriarch of the West, would limit his canonical jurisdiction
4. That the first of these councils, known as the Fourth Ecumenical Council of Constantinople held in 869, was null and void.

Despite the Pope agreeing to this, the western Catholic Church continued to abide by the first of these councils and continued to claim it as ecumenical. We examine later what was agreed to by that council.

Differences between the Greek-speaking East and the Latin-speaking West within Christendom would continue to build until 1054 when the See in Rome, Pope Leo IX, would excommunicate the East including its See in Constantinople. In return, Constantinople's Patriarch, Cerularius, would excommunicate the West and its Pope. The accusation of heretic would become thrown from each side at the other over the subsequent years.

This schism has never been healed although a gallant attempt was made from 1438–1439 at the Council of Florence. While accompanying the negotiating team from the East, Gemistus

Plethon offered lectures to the Medici household. These exciting lectures led to the founding of the Platonic Academy where young scholars and artists, such as Leonardo da Vince, studied. Plethon brought to Florence not only his wisdom expounded in lectures but also a trunk packed full of ancient texts, some of which had never been seen before in the West.

Since the time of Alexander, Egypt's Alexandria had been the world's foremost center for learning. Here were over a million sacred scrolls and texts within its libraries. Julius Caesar during the siege of Alexandria by Roman Emperor Pompey in 48 BC, apparently set ablaze the harbor warehouses wherein many manuscripts existed. But the great Library of Alexandria may not have been destroyed as some legends claim. Theodosius' son, Honorius, kept it as the most important center of learning in the Eastern empire. But he could not (or would not) control the mobs that had in 391, under his father's rule, destroyed the Temple of Serapis known as the Serapeum and the contents of its library. This library was considered to be part of the great library of Alexandria.

Here in Alexandria, the brutal execution of Hypatia happened in 415. After the previous bishop had died, savage feud broke out between the two contenders to be the next bishop, namely Orestes and Cyril. Cyril eventually wins the position perhaps aided by bribes. Cyril would be known for using bribes during his infamous career.

Because Hypatia had advised Orestes, she became a target for those supporting Cyril. The contemporary historian, Socrates of Constantinople, writes of this amazing woman in his *Ecclesiastical History*, "There was a woman at Alexandria named Hypatia, daughter of the philosopher Theon, who made such attainments in literature and science, as to far surpass all the philosophers of her own time. Having succeeded to the school of Plato and Plotinus, she explained the principles of philosophy to her auditors, many of whom came from a distance to receive her instructions. On account of the self-possession and ease of manner which she had acquired in consequence of the cultivation of her mind, she not infrequently appeared in public in the presence of the magistrates. Neither did she feel abashed in going to an assembly of men. For all men on account of her extraordinary dignity and virtue admired her all the more."[169] Other contemporaries claimed that she excelled in mathematics and astronomy. And her breadth of knowledge extended to the ancient Mysteries. In 415, a Christian mob, inspired to destroy any and all sources for heresies, seized her. They stripped her naked, then, while alive, tore off her flesh before burning her remains. Hypatia's vicious death shocked the empire and transformed her into a "martyr for philosophy."

Hypatia's death sent shockwaves throughout the empire! Christianity was about non-violence, about turning the other cheek. Leading philosophers such as Damascius became ardent in their opposition to this degenerate swell in Christianity. Philosophers now feared for their lives. Once secure from public violence, the brutal murder of their fellow philosopher, and a brilliant woman at that, caused many to seek safer schools in other lands. The exodus of scholarly and philosophical talent began to migrate from the unsafe Roman Empire eastwards where their

---

169 https://sourcebooks.fordham.edu/source/hypatia.asp

talents would lead to the blossoming of the schools around Baghdad.

The tide towards Faith over Knowledge within Christianity carried with it suspicion of every philosopher who professed Plato or Pythagoras or any Greek philosopher for that matter. And any association with the Ancient Mysteries could place a target on one's back. A feeling of "let the philosophers go" pervaded the now politically powerful Church. A Christianity for the common man motivated this impulse to overthrow the learned, the elite.

Closing of the Knowledge Stream in Christianity

Knowledge of the Logos came through Gnosticism which, when Early Christianity arrived, had been well established for some three hundred years as an outgrowth of Alexandrianism. Gnosticism and Christianity blended for a while before proto-Orthodox Christianity struggled to separate itself from dualistic philosophies. During the three hundred years it took to accomplish this separation, theological debates, sometimes deadly, raged about the Trinity, about who beget whom, about the substance for each, and about who created what. Plato and the Gnostics had claimed that a lesser God, the Demiurge, had created the physical world for Man following the Fall. This Demiurge figured into the theology of several of the Christian sects of the second century.

There were (violent) debates about the Father God. Some said that the God of the Old Testament who gave us "an eye for an eye and a tooth for a tooth" could not be the same God of love, of mercy to whom Christ prayed. Could the God of the Old Testament have been one (mere) member of the Pleroma (fullness) of the Elohim (called Exusiai in Greek in the Cosmology of Dionysius the Areopagite)? (The word "Elohim" is plural. Some esoteric groups claim there were seven Elohim.[170])

Dionysius the Areopagite defined nine layers of spiritual beings below the Godhead. Would the Trinity debates add more levels to the heavenly hierarchy? How did this hierarchy play into the human being? "It never occurred to people in those days [before the fourth century] to attribute to the human being thoughts that transmit knowledge or

---

170 http://www.spiritual-encyclopedia.com/elohim.html

perception. They ascribed those to an angel working within man. An angel inhabited the body of a human being; the angel perceived, and human being shared in this knowledge."[171]

Later, about the same time that Islam was being offered to humanity through Mohammed, Christians simplified all this to say, "there is only one God we need to be concerned with: Christ". After the seventh century, both Christianity and Islam adopted many similarities in their theologies. Were these an expression of theological truths or had materialism become the unseen, underlying, and prevailing philosophy of the times?

The Christianity that won the Heresy Wars had its roots in the Christianity brought to the West by John, son of Zebedee. But its first heresy warrior, Irenaeus, likely would not have recognized the Christianity that emerged from the fourth to the seventh century when imperial directives homogenized the nascent religion. Decrees by Theodosius I that began in 381 and continued to 391 sought at first to excommunicate any and all non-conformists

---

[171] Rudolf Steiner, lecture 16 in a series on Materialism, 3Jun1921, Dornach, GA 204

but later sought to exterminate, to root out and destroy any and all who would not openly declare their strict allegiance to the new prevailing creed. Theodosius was encouraged to issue these decrees by Church leaders.

Early Christians spoke in the first two centuries of an imminent End of the World. Dr. Rudolf Steiner explained that its leaders could sense an ending of their Logos knowledge. This 'End' happened spiritually in the fourth century according to Steiner who remarked, "the significance of the incarnation of Christ was grasped [in the first three centuries] because the power of the old [eastern] wisdom still survived. This power to grasp the significance of the Christ incarnation did not actually fade from man's faculty of comprehension until the fourth century."[172]

Similarly, Steiner pointed out, "In early Christian times until about the third or fourth century, when there was still a good deal of Oriental wisdom in Christianity, human beings occupied themselves intently with the question of the distinction between the Father God and God the Son. One could say that

---

[172] Rudolf Steiner, third lecture in a series on 4Nov1919, Bern, GA 193

these fine distinctions between the Father God and the Son God, which so engaged people's attention in the early Christian centuries, under the influence of Oriental wisdom, have long ceased to have meaning for modern man, who has been occupied in cultivating egoity. ... [modern people] take what should apply actually only to the Father God and transfer it to the Christ God. Modern theology does not actually have the Christ at all; it has only the Father, but it calls the Father Christ."[173]

What did the author of John mean when he wrote, "All things emerged through Him and without Him has emerged not one of the things that have emerged"?[174] The author is writing about Christ as the creator of the living and material world! It leaves open the question of what the Father created? The answer appears to lead us back to dualism if we answer that the Father created the spiritual world while the Christ created the physical.

The battle of Knowledge versus Faith became expressed in who had access to the Bible. St

---

[173] Rudolf Steiner, *Cosmosophy* lecture cycle, 24Sep1921, Dornach, GA 207

[174] John 1:3 (my translation), NIV: "Through him all things were made; without him nothing was made that has been made"

Jerome had intended access to the Word of God when he translated into Latin the Hebrew of the Old Testament and the Greek of the New Testament. He expected the ordinary Christians of the Roman empire should be able to read the Bible. Jerome wrote in his prologue to the *Book of Isaiah*, "Ignorance of the scriptures, he wrote, is ignorance of Christ."

But as Faith uprooted Knowledge, this perception changed in part because the people of Christian Europe spoke a language other than Latin such as German, French, Anglo-Saxon, Italian or Spanish. Such people were considered illiterate and nearly impossible to educate. Jerome's translation to Latin, known as the Vulgate, was eventually understood only by the learned who were also the monks or priests. Perhaps a pride in knowing how to read the Bible became an odd reflection of the former pride of Gnostics in their knowledge. In any case, translations into any of the European languages became forbidden.

It would not be until the fourteenth century when an English version of the Old and New Testament was produced. John Wycliffe produced an English version of the Latin Vulgate Bible in 1384. Worried that knowledge of the Bible outside the priesthood might arise, the death decree for anyone found in possession of an unlicensed English Bible was issued. But that only applied in England. Martin Luther translated the Greek New Testament to German in 1522. Emboldened, William Tyndale completed a Greek to English translation in 1525. Because writing a translation was forbidden by the Church in England, he hid and did his work in the Dutch city of Antwerp. Nonetheless, 3000 copies of his version were printed at Worms in 1526 and sent to England. When they reached port, the bishop of London seized every copy that his agents could find. They burnt almost 3000 texts at St Paul's Cross, a gathering place near the cathedral. But two copies of the original 3000 managed to survive. Eventually Wycliffe was betrayed. Authorities seized and burned him at the stake in 1536.

The Tyndale Bible played an important role in fermenting the Reformation. Its call for freedom from the corruption of the Church and for the rebirth of individual knowledge spread across the English-speaking world reaching the colonies in America and elsewhere in the British Empire. By the middle of the sixteenth century, the common person held the view that for one's own spiritual development, a personal knowledge of scripture was needed. Seventy-five years later, in 1611, fifty-four scholars produced the King James Bible. They drew significantly from the work of Tyndale.

Converting the Heathens to Christianity

Figure 14 From the Stuttgart Psalter, ninth century

Arianism and The Gothic Tribes

When Ulfilas (311 – 383) converted the Goths, the battle-loving barbarians, to Arian Christianity in the 340s, he promoted an image of Christ the Warrior. He translated the Greek bible to their Germanic language, developing the Gothic alphabet in the process. The Creed of Ulfilas, adopted by the Gothic tribes, distinguished God the Father (the "unbegotten") from God the Son (the "only-begotten" who was begotten before time *and created the physical world*), and the Holy Spirit (who proceeded from both the Father and the Son). Here is a possible source for the Filioque.

Into this Arian Christianity also streamed Celtic Christianity from Ireland.[175] But important for our topic here, is that these Gothic tribes later conquered much of Europe. As they conquered, they brought with them Arianism and the Filioque. The Great Migration of Peoples,[176] perhaps sparked by the Hun invasion, saw one of these Germanic tribes, the Vandals, carry their Arian faith into Spain and then to Carthage. In 447, the Filioque was used in Toledo, Spain. The Christian Goths overran much of the Roman Empire including the sacking of Rome by King Alaric and his Visigoths in 410. Rome would be sacked two more times in the coming two hundred years by these Arian Christians. But never did these

[175] https://en.wikipedia.org/wiki/Celtic_Christianity
[176] https://en.wikipedia.org/wiki/Migration_Period

Arians seek to overthrow the Roman Catholic Church.

The Paulicians

The sect known as the Paulicians began in 660 when Constantine of Mananalis received an initiate who put in his hands a copy of the New Testament. This initiate revealed to Constantine the mysteries inherent in its books. Deeply moved by the works of Paul, Constantine took on the name of Paul's disciple Silvanus. He felt called to restore the pure Christianity as St. Paul had taught. Using only his New Testament, he built a large following.

Twenty-seven years later, he was stoned to death as a heretic. The court official, Simeon, who had been tasked with carrying out the death order, converted to their faith. Simeon was initiated and, in keeping with the tradition, changed his name to Titus. He then took on the leadership of the sect. Eventually, its members would be declared to be Manichaeans by the Church. As Manichaeans they could be killed as heretics. Titus was subsequently seized and burned at the stake in 690. As martyrs, the sect was inspired to continue to grow.

In 747, many of the pacifist Paulicians were moved from Armenia to Thrace to act as a buffer at the Bulgarian border. In the Paulicians struggle for survival, some of them eventually trained in military skills. After 775, the Armenian Paulicians had divided into the Baanites (the orthodox party) and the Sergites (the reformed sect) who had taken up arms. By 801, the Sergites had grown powerful and henceforth led the Paulician movement.

When Byzantine Empress Theodora fought for veneration of icons, the Paulicians opposed her. For this she had 100,000 Paulicians in Byzantine Armenia slaughtered and all of their property and lands confiscated. The surviving Paulicians relocated westward to establish a State of the Paulicians at Tephrike in what today is called the Sivas Province of Turkey. In 867, the Paulician State had expanded as far as Ephesus (southwestern Turkey today). Petrus Siculus came to negotiate with the Paulicians. He stayed many months with them and from this experience wrote a book about them, *"History of the Empty and Vain Heresy of the Manichæans, Otherwise Called Paulicians."* Being associated with the Manichaean heresy proved fatal for the Paulicians. War with the Byzantine forces came, and the meager military might of the Paulicians was easily broken. However, the peaceful Paulician sects were able to retain their communities throughout the Byzantine empire. This non-violent sect is the likely source for the Bogomils and perhaps also for the Cathars.

In 970, emperor John Tzimisces forced 200,000 of the remaining Paulicians to migrate to Philippopolis in Thrace where nearly two hundred years earlier many Paulicians had been relocated. Again, they were sent to act as a Bulgarian border buffer. As a reward for their promise to keep back "the Scythians", the emperor granted them religious freedom. A revival was underway when a call for several thousand came to join the army of Alexius Comnenus against the Norman Robert Guiscard. Although the young men were conscripted, their non-violent faith led many to desert the army. This caused the emperor, in 1085, to put an end to them and their heresy. Survivors fled into Bulgaria and some continued further westward.

Like other heretics we've studied, the Paulicians believed there were two creative gods. The first one had made human soul. Later, as a result of the Fall, the other (perhaps a lesser) God then made matter and used it to fill out the human body. This likely was derived from Plato's concept of a Demiurge that was part of the Gnostic-Christian theology.

Papal Power Through Deceit

Of the Gothic tribes, the Franks play a key role in Christian history. To begin with, they were Arian and had accepted the Filioque from the Creed of Ulfilas. To them is credited the victory over the advancement of Islamic forces under Abdul Rahman Al Ghafiqi into Europe at the Battle of Tours in 732. The invaders were eventually pushed back south of the Pyrene mountains where they remained until 1492. Arab awareness of the Franks as a growing military power came only after the Battle of Tours when the Umayyad Caliph expressed shock at his army's catastrophic defeat. Had the Franks not been victorious, Leonardo's Renaissance and the Western Europe of today probably would not have happened. To the Franks, Christ the Warrior was their archetype.

Another Gothic tribe, the Lombards conquered the Byzantine capital of Ravenna in 751 under King Aistulf who then demanded the submission of Rome. Pope Stephen had been under the protection of the Roman military.

Although the Lombards were Arian, the threat to the Pope was not on religious grounds but on political. The desperate pope personally went to Pepin the Short, king of the Franks, to request his support. He showed Pepin a letter that dramatically changed the fortunes for the Church in Rome. The letter claimed that when Roman Emperor Constantine was suffering from leprosy, he had come to Pope Sylvester I. The letter stated that Sylvester converted and baptized the emperor. In gratitude, Constantine gave to the Pope "power, and dignity of glory, and vigour, and honour imperial", and "supremacy as well over the four principal sees: Alexandria, Antioch, Jerusalem, and Constantinople, as also over all the churches of God in the whole earth!" The letter further claimed Constantine bequeathed various estates "in Judea, Greece, Asia, Thrace,

Africa, Italy and the various islands." The letter

Figure 15 Charlemagne (left) and Pepin, tenth century copy of lost original from c. 830, Museo della Cattedrale

granted Popes "the city of Rome, and all the provinces, places and cities of Italy and the western regions."[177] Pepin fell for this forgery and agreed to fight his brothers, the Lombards. In return, Pope Stephen anointed Pepin in 754 in a coronation rite for French kings that lasted until 1792.

In 756, Pepin defeated the Lombard king. Then, supposedly, Pepin conferred upon the pope the "five cities" of Rimini, Pesaro, Fano, Senigallia and Ancona and their territory that extended diagonally across Italy from the Tyrrhenian to the Adriatic.

A generation later, under Desiderius, the Lombards had again taken control of much of northern Italy and Ravenna. Empowered, Desiderius then decided to reopen Lombard struggles with the current Pope, Hadrian I, who had been supporting Desiderius' rivals such as the dukes of Benevento and Spoleto. In 772, Desiderius' army entered Rome, the first Lombard king to do so. The pope had called for help from Pepin's grandson, Charlemagne who came to the rescue. Desiderius' forces were defeated at Susa, Pavia, and Verona.

---

[177] Christopher B. Coleman, "The Donation of Constantine". *Decretum Gratiani.* Part 1, Division 96, Chapters 13–14. Quoted from: *Discourse on the Forgery of the Alleged Donation of Constantine*. Yale University Press, 1922.

Desiderius surrendered in 774. Charlemagne masterfully took on the additional title, "King of the Lombards". Then, based on the forged Donation of Constantine, he offered Lombard territory to create what is now known as the Papal States.

Donation of Constantine is today known as a forged Roman imperial decree supposedly by the fourth century emperor Constantine the Great. It succeeded in transferring authority of certain territory over to the Pope. Historians accept that Pope Stephen, to win Pepin's support to fight the Lombards, had it composed. Although a forgery, it was used well into the thirteenth century in support of claims of political authority by the papacy. Even after Cardinal Nicholas of Cusa declared it to be a forgery in 1433, the Church did not acknowledge its sin.

In his philological study of the text in 1440, Catholic priest Lorenzo Valla argued that the language used in manuscript could not be dated to the fourth century. In fact, the language proved it was from the eighth century! Valla believed the forgery was so obvious that he reasoned that the Church must have had knowledge that this document was a forgery and was covering it up. Such deceit, he concluded, had “corrupted the church, caused the wars of Italy, and reinforced the "overbearing, barbarous, tyrannical priestly domination."[178] Despite such scholarly work by its own clergy, the Church continued to claim the Donation’s authenticity. We can surmise that Leonardo knew it to be a forgery and the harm it had rendered. We can surmise how Leonardo’s soul reacted to this knowledge. Finally, Cardinal and Church historian Caesar Baronius admitted that it was a forgery in his "Annales Ecclesiastici" (published 1588–1607) and the Church accepted his findings nearly a hundred years after Leonardo’s death.

Perhaps the most regrettable fallout from this forgery was that Pope Leo IX, in a letter sent in 1054 to Michael I Cerularius, Patriarch of Constantinople, cited a large portion of the document. Perhaps Leo believed it was genuine but Cerularius certainly knew better. He was, of course, incensed by this claim. This

---

[178] Peter E. Prosser, "Church history's biggest hoax: Renaissance scholarship proved fatal for one of the medieval papacy's favorite claims". *Christian History*. 20 (Journal Article): 35, 2001.

forgery contributed greatly to the East–West Schism.

In his *Divine Comedy*, written in the early fourteenth century well before Leonardo's birth, the poet Dante Alighieri wrote: "Ah, Constantine, how much evil was born, / not from your conversion, but from that donation / that the first wealthy Pope received from you!".

9. The Great Transition to One Orthodoxy

Augustine, The Philosopher of the Church

The great theologians Origen, Clement of Alexandria, Gregory Nazianzen, and Jerome, all wrestled with the transition from the ancient Mysteries to what they thought would be the new mysteries of Christianity. It is not until Augustine (354 – 430) that this transition finally comes to an end. It was especially within Augustine's soul that the battle between the old and the new was fought.

First Augustine attempted to tread a path to initiation, albeit a Manichaean[179] initiation. It proved to be only partially successful for him. He concluded that the ancient paths were no longer possible in his time. He sensed an evolution of consciousness underway. He studied the initiatory descriptions found in Plotinus, Philo, and others, but he could no longer fully free his mind from the material world as required by those initiations. Thus, he wrote, "when I wished to think of God, I could only imagine immense masses of bodies and believed that was the only kind of thing that could exist. This was the chief and almost the only cause of the errors which I could not avoid."[180] Augustine here expressed how Materialism had taken hold of the mind.

Augustine knew from his partial initiation that experiences of the spiritual could only happen when all physical senses were quieted, and the mind became free of thoughts tied to the physical. Of this he wrote, "No eyes nor ears can impart to thee what is in me. For I alone

---

[179] Manichaeans were third to tenth century Christian followers of Mani who had claimed that the Paraclete (holy spirit) worked through him.

[180] Augustine, *Confessions*, Henry Chadwick translator, Oxford University Press, 2009

can tell thee, and I tell thee in an unquestionable way." But, his inner voice, steeped in materialism, was unsatisfied with this. If full initiation was no longer possible, then how was humanity to continue to be guided, to be able to attain its divinely intended destiny?

As previously discussed, many prior texts and teachers described a blissful state achieved along the path of knowledge when one attained conscious union with God. Augustine struggled to find God this way. He wrote, "I asked the earth and she said, 'I am not it' and all that was upon the earth said the same. I asked the ocean and the abysses and all that lives in them, which said, 'We are not thy God, seek beyond us.' I asked the winds, and the whole atmosphere and its inhabitants said, 'the philosophers who sought for the essence of things in us were under an illusion, we are not God.' I asked the sun, moon, and stars, which said, "we are not God whom thou seekest.'" Augustine came to feel that God could no longer be experienced in the material creation even though it had been created by Him.

Augustine, felt strongly that the ancient Mysteries were part of a continuous stream from Adam to Christianity. He remarked that "what is now called the Christian religion already existed amongst the ancients and was not lacking at the very beginnings of the human race."[181] But what was possible in those ancient times, he realized, was no longer possible in his times. He pondered as to what could take its place.

Augustine felt himself to be at a turning point between the old world and a new one that was not yet fully formed. He struggled with the philosophical/theological questions of his time. (1) How can any theology explain the evil in the world? And (2), when the soul experiences Truth, how does it know it as Truth? Is Truth a being, a goddess, e.g., Sophia, that one experiences?

If the purpose of this world was for the good, what then is the purpose of evil? Why didn't God just create a good world and populate it with good people?

---

[181] Augustine, *Retractions* Book I, chapter 12, section 3, from *The Fathers of the Church* trans. Mary Inez Bogan, Catholic University of America Press, 1968.

And if Sophia, the goddess of Wisdom, was known as a real being to the ancient Greeks, why is she no longer experienced? Augustine explored Greek Skepticism who asked the question how do we know that we know (and what we say we know is truth)? The Skeptics concluded that one cannot know anything for certain. For a while, Augustine agreed.

From Manichaeism to Neo-Platonism to Christianity

His mother was a devout Christian and tried to raise her son as a Christian. His father was a pagan. With these polar backgrounds, Augustine, as a teen, went in search for answers.

As mentioned, Augustine tried Manichaeism which had expanded over North Africa where Augustine grew up. Manichaeism provided a path from his father's paganism to his mother's Christianity. The concepts "spirit" and "matter" made no sense for a Manichaean because these were not separate in Manichaean philosophy. What appeared to the senses was at the same time spiritual to them. Thinking united these two. The spiritual did not tower above that which presented itself to the senses. When the stars work in mystery through the sun and planets, something spiritual takes place there and here on earth at the same time. Likewise, when something material manifested, then at the same time it was also manifesting in the spiritual world. They always remain one. This became the foundation for a moral world order for the Manichaean.

Manichaeism was strong in Northern Africa where Augustine lived. But Augustine became troubled by how the religion sought knowledge as the key to salvation. Augustine came to feel that such a path is too passive and not able to effect any real change in one's soul life. Later, he would write about his experience and disappointment with Manichaeism,

“I still thought that it is not we who sin but some other nature that sins within us. It flattered my pride to think that I incurred no guilt and, when I did wrong, not to confess it... I preferred to excuse myself and blame this unknown thing which was in me but was not part of me. The truth, of course, was that it was all my own self, and my own impiety had divided me against myself. My sin was all the more incurable because I did not think myself a sinner."[182]

Skepticism helped to lead Augustine out of Manichaeism. From Skepticism he wandered to Neoplatonism. All along this path, Christianity could remain his companion.

He carried his concerns of the loss of the Mysteries with him from Northern Africa to Italy and eventually to Milan where, in 385 he received special training with St. Ambrose that "lifted the mystic veil by force of the spirit." With a new perspective about the role of the Mysteries, he could then write about the new role of faith, "the law of this tradition [the Mysteries], which consist in believing what it has not proved, is moderate and without guile. ... Who could be so blind as to say that the Church of the Apostles deserves to have no faith placed in it, when it is so loyal and is supported by the conformity of so many brethren; when these have handed down their writings to posterity so conscientiously, and when the Church has so strictly maintained the succession of teachers, down to our present bishops?" The arduous journey for Augustine

---

[182] Augustine, *Confessions*, Book V, Section 10

was entering the home stretch. The role of brotherhood in shared faith began to shine through his new works.

Augustine realized that just as the mystics of the times gone by had faith in the outcome of their initiation, so may Christians of his time must rely on faith in the Gospels.

This new way would be a path of humility, free of the pride and superiority he had experienced in some of those who had amassed knowledge. Slavery would continue to exist for many centuries and this feeling of superiority over the masses was contrary to what Augustine felt was the basis of Christianity. For him, the solution was to say that one could study as far as possible with their intellect, and from there proceed further into the spiritual world via one's faith in both the authority of the Apostolic Church and the mysteries revealed by the Gospels. One could wander through the ponderable but needed faith to grasp the imponderable.

Augustine must have wondered how long Christian faith could stand up to the forces that had, over time, debased the glory of the ancient Mysteries. What could stand up to egoism and materialism? Could anything go awry in this passing along of truth through the succession of teachers and bishops? Could evil slip into even Christianity and obscure Truth? Surely, such noble and dedicated followers of Christ could not be corrupted. He had that faith that Christianity could stand up to this evil that obscured Truth and would stand up. And if such people could be corrupted, then the sacred text, the written New Testament, was there to ward off the encroachment of any evil trying to slip into the oral teaching tradition.

A Brief History of Augustine of Hippo

Augustine grew up as a Roman in a family whose mother raised him as a Christian. He was born in 354 CE in the Roman province of Numidia in a town that is now Souk Ahras, Algeria. At the age of 11, the young Augustine was sent to a school in Madaurus. Although a brilliant student, he did not learn Greek because he disliked his brutal teacher. At 17, he went to 'college' in Carthage. There his interest in philosophy and the ancient Mysteries were piqued after studying Cicero (106 – 43 BC) who wrote, "For among the many excellent and indeed divine institutions which your Athens has brought forth and contributed to human life, none, in my opinion, is better than its Mysteries. For by their means, we have been brought out of our barbarous and savage mode of life and educated and refined to a state of civilization; and as the rites are called initiations, so in very truth we have learned from them the beginnings of life and have gained the power not only to live happily, but also to die with a better hope."[183] Augustine hoped to reconcile his mother's Christianity with his father's pagan beliefs.

In 372, at the age of 28, he entered a Manichean training that prepared him for initiation. Over the next ten years of preparation, to make a living, he taught rhetoric first in Thagaste and then in Carthage. But in 382, Manicheans come under brutal attack when Byzantine Emperor Theodosius I issued his decree of death for Manicheans. Without abandoning this faith, he moved to the relative safety of Rome where he took a teaching position. But he became disillusioned with Rome and moved to Milan in 384 after accepting a teaching position.

---

[183] Cicero, *Laws* II, xiv, 36

In 387, he befriended St. Ambrose in Milan who converts him to Christianity. Ambrose baptizes Augustine. In 391, he was ordained to serve as a priest in his former homeland, that is in Hippo Regius (now Annaba, Algeria). Four years later, he was elevated to the position of Bishop. There, in order to remove any doubts about his heretical past, he declared Christianity to be the only legitimate religion for the Roman Empire. In 398, he completed his autobiographical book, *Confessions*, which is cited several times in this book. Augustine died in Hippo Regius in 430. His writings become the foundation of Christian philosophy until the Renaissance. For this transition from Knowledge to Faith, the importance of Saint Augustine cannot be overstated.

The Holy Roman Empire

On Christmas Day, 800, Charlemagne (742 – 814) was crowned Emperor of the Romans. His eastern Frankish kingdom was known as the Carolingian Empire. Historians began to call it the 'Holy Roman Empire' in the thirteenth century in part because of its concept of *translatio imperii* that bestowed upon the emperors a supreme power claimed to be inherited from the ancient emperors of Rome.[184]

Charlemagne's Military

Charlemagne had a vision to consolidate the numerous Germanic tribes into a new empire. Over a thirty-year period beginning in 772, he defeated multiple tribes and united them under his rule. The empire grew to consist of much of present-day France, Germany, and northern Italy.

When Muslim rulers who had become established in Spain opposed one another, some turned to Charlemagne for military assistance. The invitation from Sulayman al-Arabi and Kasmin ibn Yusuf in 778, caused Charlemagne to lead his army to Saragossa, Spain. In 785, his army helped to capture Girona and Catalan. Then, in 797, his army captured Barcelona.

By 800, Charlemagne was the undisputed ruler of Western Europe. That year, on Christmas Day, Pope Leo III crowned him emperor. Charlemagne, like Pepin as king before him,

---

[184] Joachim Whaley, *Germany and the Holy Roman Empire: Volume I: Maximilian I to the Peace of Westphalia, 1493–1648*, Oxford University Press, 2013, pp. 17–20.

accepted the forged Donation of Constantine[185] as factual and thereby established the legitimacy of his crown from a papal blessing.

Militarily strong, the Frankish empire lacked culture, science, philosophy, and education. Diplomats returning from Cordoba reported on its grandeurs with hospitals, shops, schools, and streetlights. Nothing of the sort existed yet in the nascent Carolingian Empire.

Determined to bring order and culture to Europe, Charlemagne sought to be an example of a good Christian emperor. He felt that government should be for the benefit of the governed. He sought to legislate for agriculture, industry, finance, education, religion, *and morals*. His government set up money standards to encourage agricultural commerce.

But culturally Charlemagne was pushed by the Moors in Spain. The Franks lagged far behind the Islamic world in culture. Charlemagne realized that education would need to be a major part of the solution. At meals, instead of

---

[185] See Encyclopaedia Britannica, *The Donation of Constantine*, accessed 7Jul2020.

the mirth of jesters, his court listened to visiting scholars. He established centers of learning that became the inspiration for Europe's great universities. In 782, he placed Alcuin of York (735–804) as head of his newly founded Palace School in Aachen. Alcuin remained at this post until 790 when he took on envoy and ecclesiastical duties.

In 787, Charlemagne had issued a decree: there will be a school in every abbey! But who will be the teachers? And what curriculum will they use? What will be the goal of this new education? Who will be the students? With this the Carolingian Renaissance began.

Restarting the Flow of Knowledge to the West

Charlemagne sent envoys to cultural center of the world, Baghdad. Here the ruler Harun al-Rashid received them. In a show of great benevolence, he sent back the marvel of a mechanical clock along with a number of teachers. Baghdad and Cordoba were, at the time, cultural rivals. Politically astute, Charlemagne sought to align with Cordoba's rival. These gifts helped the backward West to grow out of its Gothic barbarianism.

But this new knowledge, carried from Baghdad, was soaked through with the materialism of that age. Aristotle's works in the Arabic texts had a decidedly materialistic quality. The translations from Arabic to Latin carried this quality. Alcuin of York advised Charlemagne to supplement these teachers and texts from the East by importing more Christian-Greek scholars like himself from England and Ireland. Alcuin sought for East-West balance.

The next famous teacher at the Palace School was, as Alcuin had recommended, an Irishman from England. Johannes Scotus Eriugena (815–877) whose name Scotus came from the Roman name for the Irish. In Latin, Eriu means 'Irish' and gena means 'born'. Thus, his name was Johannes the Irishman of Irish-Birth. Little is known of his remarkable education that occurred in Ireland.[186] Somehow, Eriugena was an established Greek scholar suggesting an unknown source for his education. He was recognized by his contemporaries for his Charles the Bald, Charlemagne's successor,

[186] This author wanted to explore how such educated individuals arose in Ireland and England during this era but yielded to time pressures to complete this book. Perhaps a reader will be inspired to investigate.

invited him to lead the Palace School. Eriugena moved to France in about 845.

As Alcuin before him, Eriugena continued to make the arts more than mere instruments but to connect them to the grasp of knowledge and then to the unity of wisdom. Eriugena was the first to translate many of Greek writers into Latin including Plato and Dionysius the Areopagite. He taught that all creatures, humans, angels, and devils, will eventually come to a harmonious state within God's kingdom.

Eriugena's *De divina praedestinatione* (*On Divine Predestination*, c. 851), argues against the concept of divine predestination to evil by its appeal to God's goodness, unity, and transcendence. This treatise is philosophically significant. Its dialectical analysis of key theological concepts was unique for its time. Eriugena cited Augustine's *De uera religione* to claim, "that true philosophy is true religion and conversely that true religion is true philosophy". Eriugena would also write "no one enters heaven except through philosophy". His analysis of philosophy describes its four principal parts: division, definition, demonstration, and resolution.

Adherence to this fourfold method of reasoning will lead the seeker to truth.

His students included Gilbert de la Porrée and William of Conches who later taught at the great School of Chartres. Eriugena's impact on both theology and philosophy was so great, he could be said to be the cornerstone for European schools that followed.

Harun al-Rashid

His name means Aaron the Just (or the

Figure 16 Harun al-Rashid from Arabian Nights

Upright).

Harun al-Rashid (763-809) was the Caliph, or emperor, whose capital was Baghdad. At the time of his rule, Baghdad had become the cultural center of the world. The arts, poetry, sciences, and music all flourished there.

With the Moors strong in Spain, Charlemagne sent envoys to their rival, Baghdad where Harun al-Rashid received them in 799. They offered Harun friendship. Harun, deeply pleased by this gesture, sent gifts for Charlemagne with the emissaries. Besides a mechanical clock that offered sounds and tricks every hour, he also sent scholars. The *Book of One Thousand and One Nights* is a fictional recounting of the experience in Harun's magnificent court.

On hearing of this gesture, Charlemagne's rival, Byzantine Emperor Leo IV, sought political retaliation. He encouraged the emir of Cordoba, Spain to renounce his allegiance to Baghdad. Such was the political scene at the end of the eighth century.

The Age of Pilgrimages

Of the many gifts Harun bestowed on Charlemagne, one that may be legend, was the 'keys' to Christian holy sites in Jerusalem. Within a century, thousands would journey for this once-in-a-lifetime soul-moving experience to walk the path to Golgotha or to pray at the tomb of Christ.

At first, the pilgrims' journeys were found to be beneficial not only for the soul experiences of the travelers but also for the financial gains for their hosts in the Middle East. Looking at what underlay the motivation for these pilgrimages, one finds materialism in that they sought for physical verification. It was crucial for the pilgrim to be physically present at a holy site. As this progressed, these pilgrims wanted to return with physical relics. Their Churches back home began to buy these relics (helping to cover the costs of the pilgrim's travels). As icons had won the right to be venerated, relics proved to be an important addition to the proof of Christian faith.

By the tenth century however, the journeys of the pilgrims had become treacherous. Robberies and massacres led to the call to make their path safe. Soon, the safety of the pilgrims became the justification for a crusade. The First Crusade was militarily successful and four new Middle Eastern states emerged each with a European ruler. A group of Frankish knights, sent by Pope Urban to search for the Ark of the Covenant in the ruins of Solomon's

Temple, became the Knights Templar who would set up a series of hostels for safe passage to the Holy Lands.

Western civilization, already moderately strong militarily, received a significant boost culturally and economically. Legendary accounts of heroism, chivalry, and piety (in sharp contrast to Islamic history that describe inhumane treatment and savagery by the crusaders) galvanized medieval literature and philosophy. Essentially closed for almost a thousand years, the Crusades opened the Mediterranean once again to the flow of commerce. Venice and Genoa prospered as a result. Pilgrims, under protection from the Knights Templar, were now safe in their travels. The banking system set up the Knights Templar brought not only wealth to the knights but also the envy of the European monarchs. A strong merchant class evolved. With the new wealth and power being tithed (10% of income went to the church), the Roman Church and the Pope reaped enormous benefits. But, with this newfound wealth came new forms of corruption.

Ecumenical Councils

The very first synod or council was held in year 50 in Jerusalem. Dozens followed but only seven councils became recognized by both the Roman Catholic and the Eastern Orthodox Church as legitimate and ecumenical. None of these seven were held in the western part of the Roman Empire. Each of these councils were called by the sitting Roman emperor in Constantinople thereby giving them a legal status and often military enforcement as well. Their ostensible intention was theological clarity and unity for the nascent religion, but they also were used to silence, to excommunicate, and to exterminate different theological perspectives.

During the time of Constantine's rule (306 – 337), Christianity became an accepted religion of the Roman Empire. As an emperor and politician, Constantine knew the rule of law would keep an empire in a contented state. But Christianity was already divided into multiple groups that bickered and battled with one another, each declaring the other as theologically incorrect or as heretics. Constantine wanted peace in the kingdom. Through Constantine's influence, these

Christian factions came settle their differences using governance methods of the Roman Senate.

An ecumenical council was meant to be where theological matters were resolved. Deliberations and decisions followed Roman Law. Majority voting (not necessarily truth) decided each issue. Normally the Roman Emperor convoked such a council. Delegates were to come from across Christendom (within the Roman Empire). Underlying these efforts was the desire for a single Christianity, a declaration of what the religion believed or knew to be true, that would lead to a universal and uniform religion.

Council	Date	Convoked by	President	Attendees
First Council of Nicaea	325	Emperor Constantine I	Emperor Constantine & Hosius of Corduba	318
First Council of Constantinople	381	Emperor Theodosius I	4 Patriarchs	150
Council of Ephesus	431	Emperor Theodosius II	Cyril of Alexandria	200–250
Second Council of Ephesus (not 1 of recognized 7)	449	Emperor Theodosius II	Pope Dioscorus I, Alexandria	198
Council of Chalcedon	451	Emperor Marcian	**Government** officials and senators	520
Second Council Constantinople	553	Emperor Justinian I	Eutychius of Constantinople	152
Third Council Constantinople	680-681	Emperor Constantine IV	Patriarch George I of Constantinople	300
Second Council of Niceae	787	Empress Irene as regent for Constantine VI	Patriarch Tarasius	350

In the chart above, eight successive ecumenical councils[187] show the theological progression as materialism was penetrating theology.

By exploring the topics debated at each of these councils, one can come to see the evolution towards a more materialistic perspective of the nascent religion. The sequence of topics begins with the questions of Arianism, the nature of Christ, when is Easter, ordination of eunuchs, validity of baptism by heretics, and more. Examining if Arianism was a heresy led to similar examinations of Apollinarism and Sabellianism in the second council that also debated the activity of the Holy Spirit. Following these came the decisions on Nestorianism and Pelagianism along with whether or not Mary was the mother of God (Theotokos) in 449. To cement this altered understanding, the baptism scenes of Luke and Matthew were modifed changing "today I have begotten thee" to "in whom I am well pleased." The appearance of Christ was moved back from the

[187] Derived from an article on the Seven Ecumenical Councils in Wikipedia, accessed 31July2018, https://en.wikipedia.org/wiki/First_seven_ecumenical_councils

Baptism to the birth of Jesus. But which Jesus? The prophecy of two messiahs, one kingly and one priestly, was lost. The differences in the birth stories of Luke and Matthew were glossed over so that it became but one Jesus who was Christ from birth.

This led to the debates on the nature of Jesus Christ called Hypostatic union, Monophysitism, and Monotheletism. Did Jesus have one, divine only, or two, divine and human, natures. These debates on the nature of Christ Jesus were not settled at a council. The Council of Chalcedon reversed the Second Council of Ephesus that had reached a compromise calling the nature of Christ Jesus as an amalgamation of both or miaphysite. The Nestorian church had been growing considerably in the East, so the Second Council of Constantinople continued to debate that branch while it continued to debate Monophysitism. The Third Council of Constantinople took up the question of the human and divine wills of Jesus, settling on Monothelitism. Lastly, the empress Theodora got the Second Council of Niceae to restore the veneration of icons that had been condemned by the Council of Hieria in 754.

As the pagan forms of initiation had ceased and Gnostic knowledge paths had faded, fewer and fewer individuals could still attain spiritual sight. Those who did were called mystics and viewed suspiciously as potential heretics. Earlier Councils dealt with Manichaeism, Arianism, Nestorianism, and many other variations of Christianity. By the seventh council, Orthodoxy was already in control and the question then had to do with an internal issue: icons and veneration for something material. Islam had outlawed such veneration as idolatry. Many within Christianity felt similarly and had, at the non-ecumenical Council of Hieria of 754, banned icons. The seventh ecumenical Council reinstated icons as legitimately venerable. Like icons, relics were especially venerated, and this would increase in the coming centuries with the pilgrimages to the Holy Lands.

Throughout these ecumenical councils, the Church typically succumbed to imperial whims. The earlier Second Council of Ephesus of 449, called by the Byzantine Emperor Theodosius II, was later annulled by the Council of Chalcedon. And this was, in turn, annulled by Emperor Basiliscus, who then reinstated the Council of Ephesus! Despite these imperial acts, the Second Council of Ephesus never came to be considered an ecumenical council. But the damage to the credibility of such councils had now came into question. Several councils yielded theological matters to imperial whims. The issue of fallibility thus damaged these councils. It would lead to the later designation of the infallibility of the Pope.

The Nicene Creed as of 381, read "[I believe] in the Holy Spirit, the Lord, the giver of life, who proceeds from the Father, who with the Father and the Son is adored and glorified." As compromise to admit the Arians of Spain, the Nicene Creed was altered by the Third Council of Toledo[188] in 589 to say, "We believe in the Holy Spirit ... who proceeds from the Father *and the Son*". Although this was a council within Spain that issued 23 anathemas directed against Arius, the inclusion of the Filioque infuriated the anti-Arians in the Eastern empire. The Germanic tribes had converted to Arian Christianity which had become the established theology of most of western Europe and especially of the Franks. And it was the Franks, from the time of

---

188 https://en.wikipedia.org/wiki/Third_Council_of_Toledo

Charlemagne, who protected Rome for hundreds of years. Rome likely promoted the Filioque as political payment for this protection. Contentious doctrinal issues between East and West thereby grew even worse.

The Filioque and the Great Schism

In 767, the Filioque was repudiated by a council held at Gentilly. But, in 809, Charlemagne called for a council to be held within his kingdom. The Council at Aachen was asked to confirm Charlemagne's Arian belief that the Holy Spirit proceeds from the Father *and the Son*
(in Latin, "filioque" means "and the son"). Stacked with sympathizers, the council sanctioned the inclusion in the Nicene Creed of the phrase "and the Son." The Filioque Battle within the old Roman empire now raged. The Eastern Orthodox theologians saw the Filioque as a heresy.

Pope Leo III forbade the Filioque change to the Nicene creed. To ensure it did not come up again and possibly split Christendom, he ordered in 810 that the Nicene creed be engraved on silver tablets so that it may never be overturned again.

But the issue does not go away. It festers in the former Arian territories of western Europe. In the ninth century, Photios, the Patriarch of Constantinople, accused the West of having fallen into heresy through its continued use of the Filioque. The Filioque at the Eighth Ecumenical Council became the signatory event of East-West controversy. Recall the forgery of the Donation of Constantine colored the moral aura of the Roman Church at this time.

In 1014, the Filioque clause appeared in the coronation liturgy of Emperor Henry II by Pope Benedict VIII. After the Great Schism of 1054, Filioque forces felt empowered. In 1274, the Second Council of Lyon included the Filioque in the Latin version of Nicene Creed.

The Eighth Ecumenical Council

The Eighth Ecumenical Council convened *twice* in Constantinople, ten years apart! The first was the Fourth Council of Constantinople for Catholicism. It was held in Constantinople from October 5, 869, to February 28, 870 and included 102 bishops, three papal legates, and four patriarchs. The Council, called by Emperor Basil I, met for ten sessions and issued 27 canon laws. One of these canons changed the wording of the Nicene Creed!

Controversy raged as the new Patriarch of Constantinople, Photios, opposed the new creed wording. He called the Filioque a heresy. Recall the great debates about the Trinity. These surfaced anew when Pope Nicholas I had slipped "the Filioque" into the Catholic creed, appeasing the Carolingian Franks who ascribed to this theology. The Pope, beholden to the Franks for rescuing the Vatican, apparently agreed to put this on the Council's agenda and offer it his support. With the Pope's support, it passed at the first of these two Councils.

For readers today, it is difficult to imagine how a statement that the Holy Spirit proceeds from just the Father or from both the Father and the Son could become such an intense controversy. Although this battle had already been resolved in earlier councils, this Pope reignited it. Following the first Eighth Ecumenical Council, the Nicene Creed was again changed to read:

I believe in the Holy Ghost, the Lord, the giver of life,

who proceeds from the Father and the Son who with the Father and the Son is adored and glorified.

Because of his opposition, the Council also deposed Photios, the popular Patriarch of Constantinople, and reinstated his aging predecessor Ignatius. This move opened a deep wound between the Latin and the Greek Christian worlds.

Before the Council, all five Sees (Patriarchs and Pope) were considered equals. Adding insult to injury, this Council sought to change that. It ranked Constantinople above the other three Eastern patriarchates of Alexandria, Antioch and Jerusalem, yet Rome was placed above all others. The Donation of Constantine, not known yet as a forgery, likely was cited to garner the support of the western bishops at the Council.

The Triumph of Materialism in Religion

Lastly, the Eighth Ecumenical Council dealt with the teachings from the great philosophers. For centuries, Christianity had accepted that the human soul existed as mediator between spirit and body. Such teachings claimed that a mediating soul must have two aspects: one spiritual and one earthly or mortal. When the 27 new canons were finalized, Canon #11 reduced the human being to a body and (one aspect of) soul. The second aspect of the soul was denied. Without the need of the soul to mediate for one's spirit, the human spirit itself had become anathematized! Accepted theology now limited the human to only body and soul that oversaw the body only. Materialism had quietly succeeded in slaying the spirit. The myth of Osiris had come true – the old spirit, Osiris, was dead.

The text of Canon 11 reads, "Though the old and new Testament teach that a man or woman has one rational and intellectual soul, and all the fathers and doctors of the church, who are spokesmen of God, express the same opinion, some have descended to such a depth of irreligion, through paying attention to the speculations of evil people, that they shamelessly teach as a dogma that a human being has two souls, and keep trying to prove their heresy by irrational means using a wisdom that has been made foolishness.

Therefore, this holy and universal synod is hastening to uproot this wicked theory now growing like some loathsome form of weed. Carrying in its hand the winnowing fork of truth, with the intention of consigning all the chaff to inextinguishable fire, and making clean the threshing floor of Christ, in ringing tones it declares anathema the inventors and perpetrators of such impiety and all those holding similar views; it also declares and promulgates that nobody at all should hold or preserve in any way the written teaching of the authors of this impiety. If, however, anyone presumes to act in a way contrary to this holy and great synod, let him be anathema and an outcast from the faith and way of life of Christians."[189]

The Second Eighth Ecumenical Council

In recognition of the political ramifications from deposing Photios, the emperor (not the embattled Church) reinstated him as Patriarch. Then the *'do-over'* Fourth Council of Constantinople could convene in 879–880. Because of his strong stance against the Filioque, Photios would become a saint in the Greek Orthodox Church. It was ceremoniously seen at the time as the start of a reunion of

---

189 http://www.papalencyclicals.net/councils/ecum08.htm

the Eastern and Western Churches. These two councils demonstrate the growing divide between East and West that will lead to the Great Schism of 1054.

In an attempt to keep Christendom united, the Filioque was removed but it was not explicitly condemned nor was it called a heresy. The Frankish theologians claimed knowledge on their side while their opponents relied on dogma. Hierotheos wrote of the new Frankish theologians that they "considered themselves superior to the holy Fathers of the Church and also considered human knowledge, which is a product of reason, to be higher than Revelation and experience."[190] Recall that Charlemagne, as King of the Franks, had established schools to study Greek philosophies and metaphysics. When this Council convened, his grandson, Charles the Bald, was king and proud of the growth of knowledge in his kingdom. Earlier generations of Frankish kings had had no formal education. Charlemagne put Arabic teachers to work to build an excellent educational system. By 1020 the School of Chartres was one of the leading

---

[190] Hierotheos Vlachos, *The Mind of the Orthodox Church*, transl Esther Williams, Theotokos Monastery, p. 202, 1998

schools in Europe. Great scholars were attracted to teach at the cathedral school, including Bernardus Silvestris, Englishman John of Salisbury, Thierry of Chartres, and Alanus ab Insulis. The philosophical work of these men culminated in a mini renaissance in the twelfth century that became Scholasticism. This knowledge-period was led by the works of Albertus Magnus and Thomas Aquinas whose philosophy came to dominate medieval thinking throughout Europe.

This battle of the Filioque had become an echo of the battle between Faith and Knowledge in Augustine's time. Although the Filioque was removed for the sake of reunion, it was certainly not forgotten. Once the Great Schism in the rearview mirror, the Frankish bishops reinserted it into the creed at the Council of Lyons in 1274.

The Eucharist

Sometime near to when the Eighth Ecumenical Council(s) occurred, that is, in the second half of the ninth century, the Eucharist was altered. Perhaps this was an unconscious reaction to losing the spirit in the philosophical model of the human being. As the definition of the soul had changed, the mystery of the bread and wine changed likewise. There was no longer a corollary for the wine. The bread alone sufficed for the aspect of the soul that mediated the body. Gone for the soul by theological decree was the spirit. Thus, the wine was no longer required. In the centuries preceding the ninth, both the wine and the bread were administered during the Eucharist. Now, the wine was no longer offered to the congregation.

It was claimed that one needed to be fully pure in soul, to have confessed their sins, before receiving the blood of Christ. Only the purity possessed by the priests could participate. "It is difficult to say when the practice of offering the chalice to the people stopped, but it may be presumed that this was part of the way in which Church authorities sought to prevent anything disrespectful happening to the Eucharist."[191] Another echo of the battle against Gnosticism which was declared a heresy because of its elitism in its knowledge path to divine experience. Now, ironically, the priests elevated themselves from their congregations. There arose an

---

191 https://en.wikipedia.org/wiki/Communion_under_both_kinds accessed 5Aug2018

explanation: Communion Under Both Kinds or a belief that either the bread or the wine sufficed for the Eucharist.[192] This loss of the wine helped to ferment the Reformation.

Ensoulment and Parzival

Canon #11 closed off Christian theology to Plato's transmigration of souls (reincarnation) but it raised a number of questions. Which comes first, the body or the soul? When and how does a human body acquire a soul? Is it at conception or at birth? If an infant died before receiving baptism, will it still be accepted into Heaven?

In a mystical-like response to the cessation of participation in the chalice (and to Canon #11), there arose the story of *Parzival* by Wolfram von Eschenbach (with an unfinished earlier version, *Perceval, the Story of the Grail*, by Chretien de Troyes). The popular story was about a boy who wants to become a knight. He wants to search for the Holy Grail (and the wine therein). Eventually he becomes the new Grail King. The story has connections to the singing minstrels or troubadours. Both the

---

192 https://en.wikipedia.org/wiki/Communion_under_both_kinds

story and the troubadours became very popular in the era from the eleventh to fourteenth centuries. With the Black Plague, traveling singers and storytellers ceased in Europe. Later, the story becomes the basis for Richard Wagner's famous 1882 opera *Parsifal*.

The Return of Knowledge: Scholasticism

From the Palace School to Chartres to Scholasticism

Following Eriugena's success at the Palace School, the School of Chartres soon would flower with Eriugena's students teaching there. As education spread, the way was prepared for Scholasticism to arise and from there the thirst for knowledge led to the Renaissance.

Charlemagne's education vision was largely realized during the period known as Scholasticism (1100 – 1400). The philosophies of Plato and Augustine dominated the beginning centuries of Scholasticism with Bernard of Chartres (? – 1125?), Alanus ab Insulis (Alain de Lille, 1128 – 1203), John of Salisbury (1120 – 1180), and concluding with the Franciscan monk St. Bonaventure (1217 – 1274). Next came Aristotle's philosophy which ruled the second period through the works of the Dominican monks Albertus Magnus (1200 – 1280) and Thomas Aquinas (1225 – 1274). These last three theological giants were contemporaries.

Additional contemporaries were Roger Bacon (1220 – 1292) and Averroës (1126 – 1198). Roger Bacon, an English philosopher and Franciscan friar carried Aristotelean thought to empiricism and the scientific method. Averroës, a Moor born in Cordoba, Spain, was the founding father of secular thought in Western Europe. Averroës' philosophy was decidedly Aristotelean and rejected Neo-Platonism.

During these centuries, the thirst for knowledge grew to pervade the changing culture of Europe. Just prior to the start of the Renaissance with the imminent fall of Constantinople, there came from the East more texts, more teachers, and concepts of the ancient wisdom.

Averroës and Aquinas

What Thomas Aquinas was for Western Christianity, Ibn Rushd (aka Averroës) was for Western Islam. Although the two never meet face-to-face, their respective philosophies met head-on in the thirteenth century!

Averroës (1126 – 1198) placed the mind not in the body but in the soul. He then divided the physical body from the soul's mind. Each person has a separate body giving us the illusion of being separated from the world. What is mind blends together within a universal mind. The product of our mind, our pure intellect, Averroës wrote, belonged to all humanity. He saw each human mind like cells of a cosmic single mind. When we die, our body is detached from this universal mind. Thus, what persists after death is not the individual mind because it loses its sense of separateness when it loses its body as it rejoins the universal mind.

Averroës' philosophy and his commentaries on Aristotle were translated into Latin and available throughout the schools in western Europe. The Schoolmen of Scholasticism were greatly influenced by him. His philosophy forced Thomas Aquinas and his teacher Albertus to face again the question from Augustine, "What is the relation of human reason to faith? How can the beliefs ordained by the Church be understood and upheld when reason might contradict them?"[193]

Thomas agreed that each person begins out of the universal. From life, one develops their individual nature. As an individual, we learn, we feel, and we do deeds upon the earth. After death, one then draws into the spiritual world what his universal had attracted, and his soul had made holy. Thus, one takes something of the individual with him after death.

As a scholar of Plato, Thomas likely struggled with the question of reincarnation. Although in his day he could not have discussed the pre-existence of souls, he could deal with the after-death existence of the soul. This matched the philosophical basis for Aristotle whose philosophy was dominating at this time and thus gave credence to Aquinas' philosophy.

Like Augustine, Thomas agreed that our individual intellect alone cannot attain all heights. Each individual can rise only to a certain point with his or her intellect. To go further, one must be guided by faith. What one can understand with reason and what one

---

[193] https://www.iep.utm.edu/faith-re/

feels through faith can exist together. Thus, one can come through reason to arrive at an image of God as represented in the Old Testament. But, if one wants to arrive at an understanding of Christ, one has to rely on faith because the one's spiritual experience of the human soul is not sufficient to attain to a comprehension of Christ.

Figure 17 Illustration from The Silvery Water by alchemist Ibn Umayl

The Alchemy of Aquinas

The *Aurora Consurgens* (The Coming or Rising of Dawn) hints at the coming of a new enlightenment (Renaissance). It was of the tradition of the *Emerald Tablet* written by the Egyptian Hermes Trismegistus. The oldest documentable source of the *Emerald Tablet* is the "Kitab Balaniyus al-Hakim fi'l-`Ilal Kitāb sirr al-ḫalīqa" كتاب سر الخليقة و صنعة الطبيعة أو كتاب العلل للحكيم بلنياس (book of Balanius the wise on the Causes) that was written in Arabic between the sixth and eighth centuries. This volume is attributed to "Balinas" (or Pseudo-Apollonius of Tyana).[194] In his book, Balinas frames the Emerald Tablet as ancient Hermetic wisdom. Historian Florian Ebeling records that Balinas "tells his readers that he discovered the text in a vault below a statue of Hermes in Tyana, and that, inside the vault, an old corpse on a golden throne held the emerald tablet."[195] The Balinas text is believed to be either a translation of the Egyptian original

[194] Katharine Park, Lorraine Daston. *The Cambridge History of Science: Volume 3, Early Modern Science*. Cambridge University Press, 2006. p.502

[195] Florian Ebeling. *The Secret History of Hermes Trismegistus: Hermeticism from Ancient to Modern Times*. Cornell University Press, 2007. p. 46-47, 96

into Arabic or an Arabic work written between the sixth and eighth centuries[196].

Following Balinas, a version of the *Emerald Tablet* appeared in Kitab Sirr al-Asrar (Book of the Secret of Creation and the Art of Nature). It also appeared in Kitab Ustuqus al-Uss al-Thani (Second Book of the Elements of Foundation) that is attributed to Jabir ibn Hayyan.[197] The *Emerald Tablet* was first translated into Latin in the twelfth century by Hugo of Santalla.[198] The text also appeared in a thirteenth century edition of Secretum Secretorum which, in its original was a letter from Aristotle to his student Alexander the Great.

---

[196] Nicholas Goodrick-Clarke. *The Western Esoteric Traditions: A Historical Introduction*. Oxford University Press, 2008. p. 34

[197] M. Th Houtsma. *First Encyclopaedia of Islam: 1913-1936* p. 594

[198] Florian Ebeling. *The Secret History of Hermes Trismegistus: Hermeticism from Ancient to Modern Times*. Cornell University Press, 2007. p. 49

Aquinas' *Aurora consurgens* is a commentary on the Latin translation of *Silvery Waters* by

Figure 18 Senior Zadith carries the Key that opens The Treasure House of Wisdom from Aurora Consurgens

Senior Zadith (Ibn Umayl). It also refers to the *Song of Songs (*aka *Song of Solomon)* which is an ancient text (sixth century BCE) about love and sexual longing between a man and a woman. Aquinas draws closely from it, paraphrasing many parts. *Aurora consurgens* is accompanied by about thirty-seven fine miniatures in watercolor. The illustrations are representations of alchemical symbols depicted in human or animal form. For example, mercury is depicted as a serpent, gold as the sun and silver as the moon. These illustrations incorporate some of the earliest Greek alchemical symbols known, found in the Authentic Memoirs of Zosimos of Panopolis. Clearly, alchemic knowledge was available for Aquinas to study and practice. Whatever his source, it must have escaped the attention of heresy hunters.

Mongols

A thousand years before the great Mongol empire threatened the western world, warriors of a confederation of ethnic groups called the Huns had invaded eastern Europe. Using mounted archers, their military power was effective against traditional battle techniques of Europe. Sweeping in from the Eurasian steppes during the fourth to sixth centuries, the Huns may have stimulated the Great Migration of Peoples.[199]

---

[199] https://en.wikipedia.org/wiki/Migration_Period

They contributed to the collapse of the Western Roman Empire.[200] Under Attila the Hun, they formed a unified empire. But soon after his defeat at the Battle of Nedao, Attila

Figure 19 Hulagu and his Army. Jami' al-tawarikh, Rashid al-Din. National Library of France, 1113, fol. 177

died in 453. The Hun empire then melted quickly away over the next 15 years.

---

[200] Ammianus Marcellinus, Roman History, Book XXXI, chptr. 2, http://penelope.uchicago.edu/Thayer/E/Roman/Texts/Ammian/31*.html

A millennium later, from the steppes of Central Asia, arose the largest contiguous land empire in history. The Mongol Empire, at its greatest, stretched from the Sea of Japan in the east to parts of Europe in the west. It stretched from Siberia in its north to the Indian subcontinent in its southern border.

Its great leaders are legendary including Ghenghis Khan (1162 – 1227), Möngke Khan (1209 – 1259), and Kublai Khan (1215 – 1294). Marco Polo sails to visit the court of Kublai Khan in 1266. Arriving with his father and uncle and his crew, they were treated as royals by the Great Khan who eventually asked them to go back to Europe and return with envoys who could answer some of his theological and philosophical questions. Marco Polo crew spent many years traveling with many adventures along the way. Sometime between 1271 and 1275, Marco Polo and team arrived at Kublai Khan's summer palace this time via the Silk Road. As requested, the Polos presented the Khan sacred oil from Jerusalem and papal letters with answers. They remained valued guests of the Khan for nearly twenty years. They returned to Venice in 1295. His *Book of the Marvels of the World* became better known as *The Travels of Marco Polo* (c.

1300). It is said to have inspired Christopher Columbus.

One Mongol general of particular interest to Christian history is Hulagu Khan (1217–1265). His mother was a Nestorian Christian and Hulagu considered himself a Christian as well. Hulagu's brother Möngke Khan became the Great Khan in 1251. Möngke commissioned Hulagu to spread the empire into the Islamic territories of the Middle East. There he was to found the Ilkhanate of Persia, which evolved into the Safavid dynasty, and is today the modern state of Iran.

Like other Mongol generals, relatively easy victories were experienced by Hulagu. In November of 1257, Hulagu encamped his army outside the city Baghdad. He demanded that the Caliph Al-Musta'sim surrender. The Caliph believed that Baghdad's larger army and defenses could not fall to Hulagu's forces and thus refused to surrender. Hulagu then besieged the city.

Surprising the defenders with the breaking of dikes to flood the city, then with a barrage of sophisticated artillery and then a cavalry attack caused the defenders to surrender after only

12 days. The following week saw the cruel destruction of the city and its residents. The Abbasids' vast libraries including the contents of the House of Wisdom were tossed in the rivers that subsequently turned black with ink and red with blood. The city was left depopulated. The siege is considered to mark the end of the Islamic Golden Age.

Joining Hulagu's Nestorian Christian army were other Christian forces from Armenia, Georgia, and even a Frankish contingent who came from the Crusader's remaining stronghold at Antioch. Hulagu's Nestorian Christian wife,

Figure 20: Conquest of Baghdad by the Mongols, from Rashid al-Din's Gami' at-tawarih, Stootsbibliothek, Berlin, 14th C.

Dokuz Khatun, persuaded her husband to spare the lives of Baghdad's Christian inhabitants. Hulagu offered the royal palace to the Nestorian Christian Mar Makikha and ordered a cathedral to be built for him. For the Islamic world, the loss of Baghdad was a severe blow. And the brutality of the Christian victors has often been mentioned in religious debates when the Christian side attempts to position its history as cultured and non-violent.

When Marco Polo arrived, during the thirteenth century, the Mongol Empire had already become the largest contiguous land empire in history. Later, Kublai Khan would separate his empire into four separate khanates: The Golden Horde Khanate in Russia, the Chagatai Khanate in Central Asia, the Ilkhanate in the Middle East, and the Yuan dynasty in China. In 1368 the Han Chinese Ming dynasty defeated the Mongol khanate in China forcing the Genghis rulers of the Yuan to retreat to the Mongolian homeland. There they ruled as the Northern Yuan dynasty. The Ilkhanate of the Middle East disintegrated in the period 1335–1353. The Golden Horde Khanate lasted until 1480 when it was defeated and thrown out of Russia by the

Grand Duchy of Moscow. The Chagatai Khanate lasted until 1687.

Survey of Medieval Heretics

Paulicians

Earlier the cruel fate suffered by the Paulicians was mentioned. We saw that many avoided

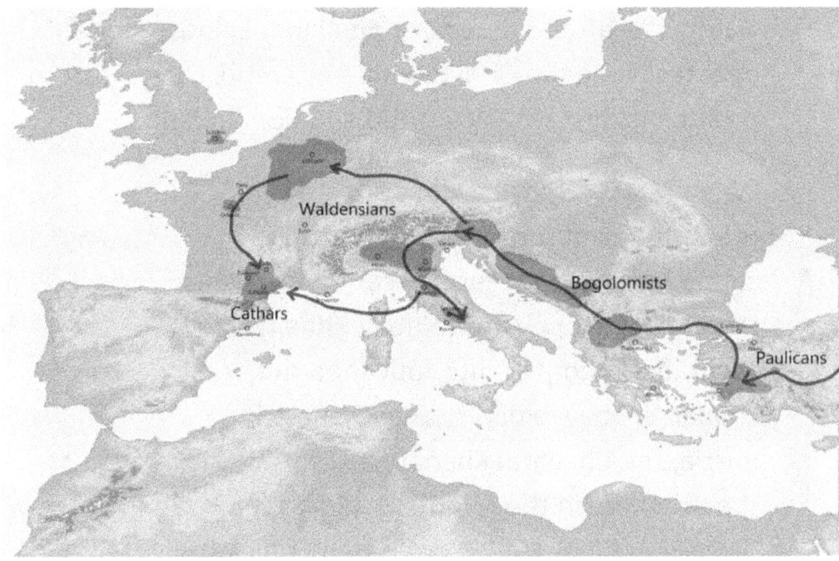

Figure 21 Spread of Paulicanism (and Manichaeism)

being slaughter by fleeing into neighboring Bulgaria. Historians trace the Bogomils back to Armenia where this group known as the Paulicians originated in about 650.

Bogomils

Historian Dimitry Obolensky wrote, “The study of the Bogomil movement has its own, and by no means negligible, part to play in the investigation of the cultural and religious links between eastern and western Europe, the importance of which is increasingly perceived at the present time."[201] These Bogomils resided in what is today called Bulgaria and Bosnia.

Their name means "dear to God." With Catholic and Orthodox interests competing in repressive ways for control of the population, many of the Bulgarians and Bosnians looked favorably upon the Christian Bogomils. Because of the weariness from constant war in the Balkan area, the Bogomils were seen by their compatriots as more attuned to the Christian faith than either the Roman Catholic or Serb Orthodox churches. Both Catholics and Orthodox persecuted the Bogomils as heretics but this only proved to increase their valor with martyrdom. Their demise would come when the Ottoman Empire overran the region in 1463. These Bosnians were more likely to convert to Islam than to join either the western or the eastern Church.

---

[201] Dimitry Obolensky, *The Bogomils: a Study in Balkan Neo-Manichaeism*, Cambridge, 1948

Like other so-called heretics, Bogomil literature and relics were destroyed by those who condemned them. Writings of the tenth century Bulgarian official Cosmas, or those of twelfth century monk Euthymius Zigabenus, if factual, show that the Bogomils believed that God created Mankind's soul in the beginning. Humans once lived for a long while in a paradise until Eve was seduced by Lucifer. To balance out what Lucifer brought to humanity, God's eldest son, Satan, was called upon to create out of darkness the world of matter. There the corrupted Adam and Eve stream of humanity was cast in order to work through the "gift" from Lucifer.

Cathars

This Christian brotherhood sect moved across western Europe and became known by various names. In France, they were known as the Cathars. The name, Cathar, came from John's gospel where it described the baptism by fire. Katheroi is Greek for such a purification, a purging that left one liberated from the clutches of the flesh and matter. Thus, the Cathars were devotees of John the Evangelist. In their cloaks they carried a copy of John's gospel at all times.

Their settlements in southern France became very popular. Languedoc grew to become a center for the Cathar economic and cultural integration. Cathar skills and trades brought economic prosperity to once poverty-stricken regions thereby garnering them love and respect of the populace.

Life of the Cathars

They lived simple lives based on freeing themselves from desires for earthly riches and attachments. They were vegetarians known for their knowledge of herbs for both cooking and healing. They strived for harmonizing with nature rather than defeating her. They were known for skills in weaving and in alchemy.

Their society was based on equality of all before God. Wealthy and poor mixed without classes. Equality extended to the sexes. Because of the power of sexuality upon the flesh, they had separate but equal ministries for men and women. Their cultured and educated society was democratic and stressed brotherhood, community, and virtues in dealings with others.

The Cathars were skilled in music and musical instruments. Their songs and poems celebrated Chivalry and the path to a higher union with Sophia (divine wisdom). They may have been the source for the beloved troubadours.

Perhaps the most admired of their traits by the outside populace was their authentic striving for self-transformation. Like early Christians, they had a secret path of initiation. Their initiates were called Perfecti (recall the use of the term *Perfect* in Early Christianity). Perfecti men and women traveled as pairs throughout southern France offering personal and community assistance, brotherhood, and wisdom.

Theology of the Cathars

In their communities, mysticism and a kind of neo-Gnosticism flourished. Their theology was akin to the once vibrant understanding of the Cosmic Christ in Manichaeism. As pacifists, they had no military. They shunned all violence. Killing any living thing was forbidden, hence they were vegetarians. Lies were seen as a kind of spiritual crime. Similarly, the swearing of oaths was abhorred. As did the Manichaeans before them, they sought to transform evil through the power of love.

In their theology, the Christ could be within one. Once within, Christ became their "I am," their higher self, in the spirit of St. Paul who said, "no longer I, but Christ in me." Thus, one did not need a priest (who the populace was increasingly seeing as corrupt) as an intermediary to Christ or to God. Like the Donatists,[202] they felt that when a ritual such as the eucharist was enacted by a corrupt priest, it was not valid.

They accepted reincarnation (which, by the fourth century, had been formerly abolished by the Church). They felt it could take multiple incarnations to fully walk the path to Perfection. Christ had come to help mankind find a new way home. Humans would become like angels when perfected.

Like the Manicheans and other dualists, they felt that the material world was created by the Demiurge and not by The Father. Along with the darkness, there was a good heaven and there was goodness on the earth. Each human being was given from the divine fire a spark as their inner light. This gave them their free will and the freedom to choose evil or good.

---

[202] See https://en.wikipedia.org/wiki/Donatism

Initiates could perceive the good spiritual world, they called Arcadia. For an initiate, it was said to be more real than the evil-filled physical world.

Cathars believed that only Jesus' body had died on the cross, but Christ, a God, was an immortal being. The cross to them was a symbol of mortality, of the lower nature of man. Fourteenth century Cathar Perfect Pierre Authié wrote, "just as a man should with an axe break the gallows on which his father was hanged, so you ought to try and break crucifixes, because Christ was suspended from it, albeit only in seeming."[203] This view rings of the dualism of Manichaeism.

After the crucifixion, what would be the body (and blood) of Christ? Because Christ's blood had entered the earth from which all things, e.g., grain and grapes, are grown, then to the Cathars the Eucharist did indeed represent Christ's body and blood. The earth had become His body and the waters, the saps, the juices, His blood. But, for them, the mass, because it was celebrated by corrupt priests, had lost its meaning.

---

[203] https://en.wikipedia.org/wiki/Cathar_yellow_cross

They did not dispute that the mother of Jesus was the Virgin Mary, but for them the mother of Christ was Sophia (wisdom). Hence, they would not accept the *theotokos* (mother of God) concept. For the Cathar, the virgin birth of the Christ can happen in each soul but only through a purified soul. This virgin birth was one's higher self. Baptism was symbolic of the purification. At the Baptism, the Christ spirit, like a dove, could descend and remain upon Jesus of Nazareth.

The Albigensian Crusade

When word of the Cathars' Church corruption claims reached the bishops, they felt they could no longer tolerate this Christian sect. In May of 1208, the Bishop of Citeaux, Arnaud Amaury, and the local clergy formed an army of northern knights. These were inspired to be a Crusade against evil. Begun in Albi, France, it became known as the Albigensian Crusade.

Their first easy target was Quercy. The pacifist Cathars could offer no military opposition. The "army" with their bishop's approval then marched toward Toulouse plundering, murdering, raping, setting fires, destroying crops, farms, and villages on their way. They came upon Beziers, a large Cathar city. On the outskirts, when asked how each crusader could distinguish between the (good) Catholics and the (evil) Cathars, Arnaud Amaury infamously answered, “Kill them all, God will recognize His own!”

Coincidentally, that day happened to be a celebration day for the Cathars. 7000 were kneeling and praying in their church as the crusaders entered the building. All 7000 died without any resistance. Amaury bragged gleefully to Pope Innocent III writing, "Today your Holiness, 20,000 heretics were put to the sword, regardless of rank, age, or sex.”

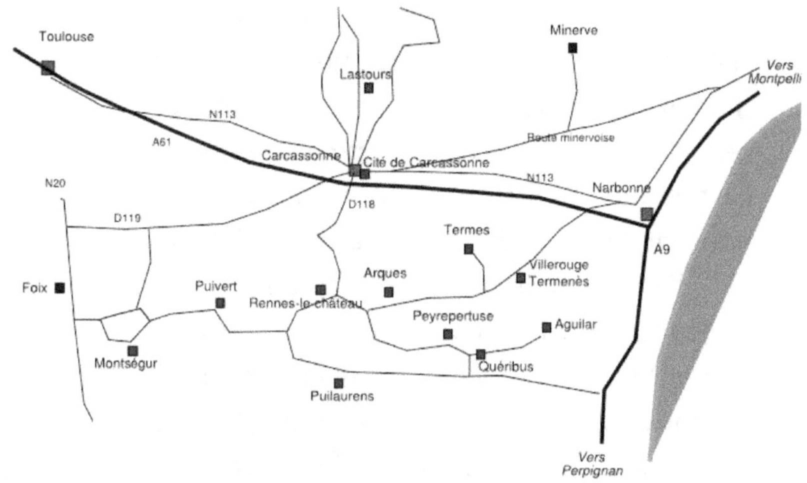

Figure 22 Map of Cathar Chateaux sites

Historian Zoe Oldenbourg wrote that after Beziers, many of the troops felt remorse. The Crusade was in danger of a moral collapse. So, Arnaud Amaury gave the leadership of this Crusade to Simon de Montfort. Simon's coat of arms was a lion with the forked tail. He was recruited because of his reputation as being intensely cruel. It was written that he felt great joy at seeing mass executions.[204]

---

[204] Zoe Oldenbourg, *Massacre At Montsegur: A History Of The Albigensian Crusade*, Weidenfeld & Nicolson, 2015

Just over two months after Beziers, in August 1208, Simon attacked the undefended town of Carcassone. Similarly, he stated, "God will know his own." Simon pushed his troops on to the next town Bram where, of those captured, he ordered the knights and mercenaries not to kill them but to first slit the captured Cathar's noses and lips. Next, he ordered the soldiers to lop off their hands, ears, and feet, and finally to gouge out eyes. He then released them so that all would greatly fear these Crusaders. Oldenbourg describes how hundreds of blind, mutilated men, women and children were led by a surviving but one-eyed Cathar to next town to show the consequences of heresy.

During this Crusade, tens of thousands were either massacred or burned alive. Their only refuge being Templar houses and castles or fleeing to the forests. This cruel crusade lasted for fifteen years!

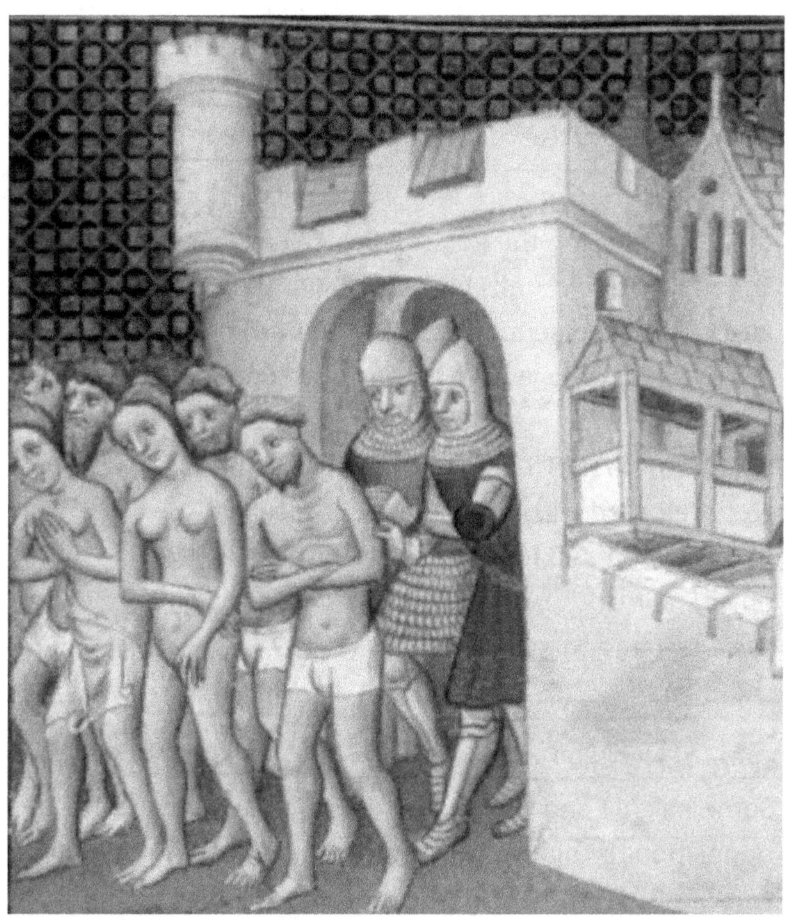

Figure 23 Cathars being expelled from Carcassonne in 1209, Boucicaut Master, Grandes Chroniques de France

Initiating the Inquisition

When there seemed to be no Cathars left alive, Pope Gregory, ordered an Inquisition to root out any survivors or sympathizers. He placed the Dominican monks in charge of the Inquisition. Their role would eventually spread across Europe. These Dominicans derogatorily became known as the 'Domini Canni' or "the hounds of God."

Franciscan monks were later added to this task thereby debasing the goals of Saint Francis. Together these monks had the power to interrogate and send any person to burn on the pyre who was even only *suspected* of being a Cathar or even just a Cathar protector. Repentant first offenders (of being a Cathar) were released with the penance to: "carry from now on and forever two yellow crosses on all their clothes ... to be worn in front on the chest and the other between the shoulders"

Were There Any Who Protected the Cathars?
Some knights and fiefdom leaders did present opposition to this crusade, but their opposition was easily defeated. Did the morally endowed Knights Templar come to their aid?

The moral authority of the Knights Templar had already been ruined with the Sack of Constantinople in 1204 (the siege began in 1203 by the Fourth Crusaders). It brought shame upon the Knights Templar for joining with these Crusaders who looted the defeated city. Despite their oaths, the Knights did not prevent Constantinople's holy sanctuaries from being violated and pillaged. Altars were smashed for their gold and marble. The Crusaders destroyed or stole all they could lay their hands on. These stolen items they sold back home to their Church in order to finance their Crusade to the Holy Lands. While the Knights may not have joined in the looting, they had enabled it through their involvement.

The Knights had sworn to fight in service of Christendom without question. But when many thousands of Constantinople's citizens were killed in cold blood and most of the women, even nuns, were raped in the lust for spoils, the Templars could no longer win in battle. Their enemies no longer feared these warriors. Their moral stature was broken. They could not protect the Cathars although they may have sought safety in their castles. There is no record of their offer to protect the Cathars and their Christianity.

Montsegur

The last major stronghold for the Cathars was Montsegur. A sizable force of mercenaries was headed by King Louis of France. After 20 years of Inquisition and Crusade, there was nothing of the Cathars left save its citadel of Montsegur. As the army marched there, over 200 surviving Cathars fled into the citadel overcrowding its capabilities. The siege lasted 10 months. The Cathars surrendered. They were given 15 days to prepare to burn in a bonfire.

The Treasure of Montsegur

In those 15 days they fasted and prayed and prepared to save their treasure. Legend alleges that this treasure was a child who their initiates knew to be important for humanity's future. The child would one day, in its next life, become Christian Rosenkreutz.

Figure 24 Cathar Chateaux of Montsegur

One night, as the mercenary soldiers and mob awaited the burning of these last Cathars, four members led the child to safety. They scaled down Montsegur's cliff using ropes and underground passageways to escape. They traveled to a Templar sanctuary. One legend placed this near the Pyrenees while another placed it in a Bogomil community where the child would receive his education and training.

According to historian Maurice Magre (1877–1941) in his book Magicians, Seers, and Mystics, this child had already escaped one disaster.[205] "He was the last descendant of the Germelshausen, a German family which flourished in the thirteenth century. Their castle stood in the Thuringian Forest on the Border of Hesse. They had embraced Albigensian (i.e., Cathar) doctrines with their Gnostic-Christian beliefs. The whole family was put to death by Konrad von Marburg except for the youngest son, who was only five years old. He was carried away secretly by a monk who was an Albigensian adept from Languedoc. The child was placed in a monastery which had already come under the influence of the Albigenses. Here he spent his early boyhood. And here he made the acquaintance of the four other brothers who were later to be associated with his escape and in the founding of the Rosicrucian Brotherhood."[206]

On the 16th of March 1244, the remaining 215 Cathars, singing and holding hands, descended from the citadel to be burned. Their joy

---

[205] Maurice Magre, *Magicians, Seers, and Mystics*, Kessinger, 1997

[206] https://en.wikipedia.org/wiki/Christian_Rosenkreuz

dumbfounded the soldiers who afterward called the field where the pyres were, the Field of the Cremated.

10. Renaissance: Knowledge Coming of Age

We've explored some of the history leading up to the Renaissance. We saw the thirst for knowledge which died late in the fourth century, was newly conceived with Charlemagne. With scholars from West and East, the European educational system was birthed leading to the Great School of Chartres and then to Scholasticism. Like an infant growing up become a teen, Knowledge entered flamboyantly into the Renaissance period. Several individuals can be said to be catalysts for this new period of learning, for they opened doors to concepts and history hitherto unknown to European scholars.

Manuel Chrysolorus, Invocator of the Renaissance

Manuel Chrysolorus (1355 – 1415) arrived in Italy in 1391 as an envoy to the West from Constantinople. His goal was to secure military help for Christianity in the East. While in Italy, he gave lectures on Greek philosophers. One of his students was Roberto de' Rossi who later became Cosimo de' Medici's tutor.

In 1396, he was invited to teach at the University of Florence. Four years later, he accepted requests to teach at Bologna, Venice, and Rome. This groundwork prepared the soil for what would spring to life in the Renaissance. He inspired scholars to go on missions to save ancient texts in the East. With the destruction of Baghdad in 1258, it was realized that any great center of learning could fall to a conqueror. The destruction of the texts of heretics was not limited to the West. Texts of Eastern and Early Christianity were in danger of destruction.

Manuel Chrysolorus knew a short period of time remained to save this knowledge. Constantinople was weak and most could see its demise was coming soon if it could not secure military assistance.

In 1423, Giovanni Aurispa returned to Italy with some 238 texts including works unknown to Europe from Plato, Plotinus, Proclus, Sophocles, Aeschylus, and more. Then in 1469, Basilios Bessarion brought to the Library of San

Marcos in Venice more than 800 volumes from the East.[207]

G. Gemistus Plethon, Catalyst for the Renaissance

In 1428, Byzantian Emperor John VIII asked the empire's wisest man, Gemistus Plethon (1355 – 1452), to join the team of envoys from Constantinople for the upcoming Council of Florence. The primary goal of this council was the mend the Great Schism of 1054. Besides the attempt to reconcile this East-West schism, emperor John VIII was also seeking European help against the Ottomans. The emperor had asked Plethon to accompany him because of his renowned wisdom and morality. I suspect there was more than his reputation for wisdom and morality. Likely he was recognized as an initiate. Although Plethon was not a practicing Christian, John often had discussed with him how the split churches can be unified. John trusted him and hoped that Plethon could help to build a new East-West bridge.

---

[207] Peter D'Eprio, *The Book of Firsts*, pg. 337-338, and Peter Liebregts, *Ezra Pound and Neoplatonism*

The Council of Florence 1438 - 1439
While in Florence, Plethon offered lectures on Plato. These were so exciting to the intellectuals of Florence that Cosimo de' Medici decided to set up an Academy in Florence and asked Plethon to lecture there. His lectures on the differences between Plato and Aristotle created a passion for Greek philosophies. Plethon summarized these lectures in his book *On the Differences of Aristotle from Plato.* But the scholars clamored for more.

Because of what he inspired, we can give Plethon the title, the Catalyst for the Renaissance. The Florentines called him a "Prince Among the Philosophers." We hear the remnants of reincarnation in the words of Marsilio Ficino who called him "the second Plato". Even the local Cardinal Bessarion wondered, "Is Plato's soul in this body?". Besides Greek philosophies, Plethon was well versed in Neo-Platonism, Egyptian mystics such as Hermes Trismegistus, Persian Zoroastrism (Zarathustra), and the ancient Mysteries. Among the books in the trunk full of texts were some by Hermes Trismegistus that were likely the source for Ficino's *Orphic System of Natural Magic*.[208]

Plethon believed that the West had been influenced by Arabic (materialistic) interpretations especially those of Aristotle (recall Harun al-Rashid's gift to Charlemagne included Arabic texts of Aristotle that were subsequently translated into Latin). Plethon argued strongly against this interpretation of Aristotle.

Plethon loved and practiced the ancient Greek paganism. He believed it was a spiritually rich prelude to Christianity. He encouraged a team assigned by de' Medici to translate the books in his trunk. The Byzantines had more access to the ancient wisdom and had in their possession many other texts that the West had either hitherto not seen or had lost sight of. His Florentine work inspired the Renaissance paintings that portrayed depictions of Greek mythology as explorations of their relationship to certain Biblical passages.

After the council ended, unsuccessfully for John VIII, Plethon remained for an additional

---

[208] Frances Yates, *Giordano Bruno and the Hermetic Tradition*, Univ. of Chicago Press, 1964

year training those who would become teachers. Plethon's role was, thereby, continued by those he trained at what would become the Platonic Academy. In 1440, Plethon journeyed to his beloved Greece to found a mystery center in Mystra. In order to offer a mystery center, he obviously must have known how to administer initiation practices as a hierophant. Plethon died there in 1452, the same year in which Leonardo was born. Plethon obviously was much more than just a great teacher as evidenced by the dramatic and dangerous decision fourteen years after his death by some of his Florentine students to sail to Mystra and steal his remains. These were reinterred in the Tempio Malatestiano of nearby Rimini "so that the great Teacher may be among free men." Surely Plethon was an initiate already during his time in Florence as only an initiate could found a true Mystery Center.

Sometime after Plethon's departure, the exact year is not known, the Accademia Platonica became established with Florence's top philosopher, Marsilio Ficino as its head. "To expound the works of Ficino is to write the history of Platonism in Italy... the Academy came into being and died with him"[209] in 1499. No known documents describe the exact nature of this academy between the time of Plethon's lectures and Ficino's appointment. But given the Platonic concepts plus those of other mystics, participants and lecturers needed to keep open an eye and an ear for the Inquisitors.

Leonardo da Vinci and the Platonic Academy

When Leonardo was 10-years old, Marsilio Ficino was already leading the Platonic Academy. Leonardo knew Ficino well – he painted him! Thus, Leonardo would know Ficino's philosophy such as, "He alone uses each thing well who has learned of his own power and that of others, from wisdom." The other great teachers at the academy were

---

[209] Pasquale Villari, *Niccolo Machiavelli*, Firenze, 1877

available to Leonardo including,

Figure 25 From Annunciation of the Angel to Zaccharia. shows Marsilio Ficino (left), Cristoforo Landino (2nd), Angelo Poliziano (3rd), and (4th) Demetrius Chalcondyles

- John Argyropoulos, an Aristotelian from Constantinople,
- Pico della Mirandola, a philosopher who founded Christian Kabbalism, developed Western esotericism, was an expert on religion, philosophy, and magic, wrote the *Oration on the Dignity of Man*, which became known as the "Manifesto of the Renaissance." His *900 Theses* was banned

by the Church. Pico certainly would have been punished as a heretic were it not for his support from the powerful Lorenzo de' Medici.

- C. Landino, who was a member of the Platonic Academy, prepared commentaries on the Greek philosophers, and worked with Marsilio Ficino. He was the tutor of Lorenzo de' Medici and his brother Giuliano.
- Angelo Poliziano was a scholar, a professor, and a poet. He had students draw their ideal of life from the ancient wisdom.

Florence as a Hub of Mystery Wisdom

Florence had been home to a thriving community of Cathars. In part, because of witnessing their terrible fate, secret schools existed where mysticism and heretical concepts could be learned and discussed. These are hinted at but not recorded by recorded by history.

What did one learn at this Academy and in fifteenth century Florence? Certainly, one explored Greek mythology and philosophy and the Ancient Mysteries. Did this extend into a study of the theologies of Early or Eastern Christianity? It must have made a deep impression on Leonardo da Vince, for he established a similar Academy in Milan.

Renaissance: A Rebirth of Greek Philosophy

As the Renaissance got underway, the

Figure 26 Insignia of the Templar Knights

"Hounds of God" were still seeking out and burning so-called heretics. Those who were interested in the ancient Mysteries and even in Platonism were considered possible heretics. Besides an outer pressure for secrecy, the ancient rule against divulging a Mystery Center's secrets to the uninitiated gave inner requirements for secrecy.

Various groups had carried Greek and Mystery knowledge to Europe. We saw that Charlemagne helped to restart the flow from East to West. With great effect, the Kabbalists brought Jewish esotericism to Europe. The Cathars and the Bogomils contributed to the rebirth of knowledge especially in regard to

Greek philosophy and Christian esotericism. The infrastructure of the Knights Templars allowed for a more open stream to flow. When their order was tortured and destroyed by Philip IV, some fled to Scotland where they founded esoteric rites for Freemasonry. And just before the Renaissance began, the Rosicrucians arose secretly within Europe. They developed a new form of initiation for westerners.

Throughout the middle ages, alchemists and Hermeticists were secretly and not-so-secretly working. Florentine art increased interest in Neoplatonism. Artists explored themes that related Greek mythology to events in the life of Christ. Interestingly, during this time, Greek statues from Roman times were excavated from underground.

Renaissance artists such as Leonardo da Vinci learned a lot about Plato, Aristotle, and other Greek philosophers from the Accademia Platonica of Florence. From the many hundreds of texts brought to Florence, these artists also learned a great deal about the ancient Mysteries and Gnosticism. As the Renaissance began, Religion and Art were not yet separated. The Florentine art schools wanted to reveal Beauty in their works and struggled with how to also reveal the ugliness of humanity. Should the suffering savior be depicted with a divine glow emanating from within? Should He, as a divine being becoming a human, wear a beard? How could their paintings depict that which came from another world?

Cimabue (1240 – 1302) and his pupil Giotto (1267 – 1337) faced these issues. For them, it was important to show how this other world had come down to be revealed in the mineral earth. Selecting babies as innocent, as freshly arrived from a spiritual world solved some of these issues. A young, virgin Madonna also helped.

Figure 27 Cimabue fresco in Lower Basilica of Assissi

Resistance to the Renaissance

In addition to concerns about the Inquisition, Renaissance painters and scholars had other concerns for their well-being. Foremost here was the rise to power of Girolamo Savonarola (1452 – 1498), a Dominican friar and preacher. In 1482, when both he and Leonardo were 30-years old, the friar called for a Christian renewal. His popularity swelled as he denounced clerical corruption, despotic rule, and the exploitation of the poor.

Figure 28 Girolamo Savonarola by Fra Bartolomeo, 1498, Museo di San Marco

His movement grew sufficiently strong that his followers sought to expel the ruling Medici and establish a popular republic. They succeeded in sending the Medici into exile and declared Florence to be the New Jerusalem.

Savonarola then instituted a puritanical campaign that began in 1482. He enlisted the Florentine youth to seek out and publicly burn all art "intended for the vain". That same year, Leonardo da Vinci left Florence for the safety of Milan. Milan's duke hired the now highly respected master artist to a post as court artist. Leonardo traveled with his paintings. We do not know how many there were, but as we've seen, one was his nearly complete *Virgin of the Rocks*.[210]

Leonardo da Vinci's Own Platonic Academy

Within three years after his arrival in Milan, Leonardo had established his Academy. He wrote over its entrance, as Plato had, "Let no one enter here who is lacking in geometry." Students enrolled primarily to study art and design with the great master, but also the Academy was famous for its mathematics, sciences, and philosophy. In addition to pupils Ambrogio de Predis, Bernardino de' Conti, Giampietrino, Cesare da Sesto, Giovanni Antonio Boltraffio, Francesco Napoletano, Andrea Solario, and Marco d'Oggiono, a circle of artists grew around the master and these included Bernardino Luini, Bernardino Lanino, Giovanni Francesco Rustici, Cesare Magni, Il Sodoma (Giovanni Antonio Bazzi), and Martino Piazza da Lodi. Flemish and northern European artists traveled to learn in the art schools in

---

[210] Andrew Linnell, The Hidden Heretic of the Renaissance: Leonardo, Amazon, 2020

and around Milan. These included Albrecht Dürer and Joos van Cleve.

As Walter Isaacson wrote in his biography of Leonardo da Vinci, "he began pursuing anatomy as a scientific as well as an artistic endeavor. But he did not regard these as separate."[211] This was how these subjects were treated in the Platonic Academy of Florence. The great mathematician, Luca Pacioli, was invited to teach at Leonardo's Academy in 1492.

For seven years Leonardo's academy flourished, but, in 1499, came the Second Italian War. When French troops marched into northern Italy, Leonardo took his paintings and fled. Infamously, the French troops used his massive but unfinished Horse statue for target practice during the First Italian War. As a refugee, Leonardo moved from place to place until he settled again in Florence which was now safe for him after Savonarola had been burned in 1498. Savonarola had lost popular favor when he refused to send troops to help defend against the first French invasion. Later

---

[211] Walter Isaacson, *Leonardo da Vinci*, Simon and Schuster, 2017

while imprisoned and under torture, he confessed to making up some of his visions.

Florence was no longer the Florence Leonardo once knew. Thus when, in 1515, an invitation came, he accepted and moved to Rome. But Rome was not to his liking either. A year later, King Francois I of France offered him a commission as chief painter, engineer, and architect to the King. The position came with a magnificent chateau in Clos Lucé, France. Here he would remain friends with the King until he died on May 2, 1519 at age 67.

11. The Reformation

We've explored a cruel and corrupt history of Christianity that was administered largely by the Church in Rome but also by the Church in Constantinople and by imperial decrees. We saw the battle between Faith and Knowledge during the Age of Augustine. All during this time we saw the transition from the wisdom of the ancient Mysteries in the few to the general intellect of the many, albeit a materialistic intellect. The understanding of Christ from the Cosmos who entered for three years the body of Jesus of Nazareth was lost.

The many Christianities of the early years of Christianity had given way to a call for one, uniform religion. The truths of the new religion were settled by majority vote. Stacking the vote became common as corruption and cruelty to opponents sunk into the soul of the Church (both in Rome and Constantinople). The use of imperial might to subdue different opinions became an all-too-frequent option.

Stacking the bishops with those who agreed with your theology transformed into powerful families placing their sons into the Church's positions of power. Corruption set in. Kings tried to control the Pope or the Patriarch. Religion bowed to Imperial might.

Theological debates that seem trivial to judgments today, led, in their times, to massive exterminations. Dogma ruled. As Knowledge had been born again, it wanted to throw off these chains as the Renaissance got underway. As the Church fought back using the terms of heresy to quell the Knowledge uprising, the Reformation became a natural outcome.

Henry VIII and the Reformation in England

King Henry VIII of England was a devout Catholic. But his attempt for Church approval to annul his marriage with Catherine of Aragon who could not bear him a son and for him to marry Anne Boleyn led him to cast out the unpopular Catholic Church in England and establish himself as the head of the new Church of England. The story of the Reformation is well documented. We've explored how the murder of Jan Huss led to the he Bohemian Reformation and how John Wycliffe's translation of the Bible gave to the budding intellect the feeling it no longer needed the Church to interpret the texts.

Instead, here we'll examine some side stories to feel the mood of the times. The following story proposes that Leonardo da Vinci likely met Henry VIII's second wife Anne Boleyn.

"Anne was the daughter of Thomas Boleyn, 1st Earl of Wiltshire, and his wife, Lady Elizabeth Howard, and was educated in the Netherlands and France, largely as a maid of honor to Queen Claude of France. ... a letter Anne wrote sometime in 1514, she wrote it in French to her father, who was still living in England while Anne was completing her education at Mechelen, in the Burgundian Netherlands, now Belgium. ... Anne returned to England in early 1522, to marry her Irish cousin James Butler, 9th Earl of Ormond; the marriage plans were broken off, and instead she secured a post at court as maid of honor to Henry VIII's wife, Catherine of Aragon.

Early in 1523 Anne was secretly betrothed to Henry Percy, son of Henry Percy, 5th Earl of Northumberland, but the betrothal was broken off when the Earl refused to support their engagement. Cardinal Wolsey refused the match in January 1524 and Anne was sent back home to Hever Castle. In February or March 1526, Henry VIII began his pursuit of

Anne. She resisted his attempts to seduce her, refusing to become his mistress, which her sister Mary had been. It soon became the one absorbing object of Henry's desires to annul his marriage to Catherine so he would be free to marry Anne. When it became clear that Pope Clement VII would not annul the marriage, the breaking of the Catholic Church's power in England began. In 1532, Henry granted Anne the Marquessate of Pembroke.

Henry and Anne formally married on 25 January 1533, after a secret wedding on 14 November 1532."

Leonardo da Vinci was in Milan from 1482 to 1499 when he became a refuge from the Second Italian War with France. Finally, in 1503 he returned to Florence. In 1506 he was legally obligated to return to Milan. He then bounced back and forth between Milan and Florence until 1513 when he was invited to Rome. In 1516, King Francis I of France who had recaptured Milan a few months earlier in 1515 invited him to take on a house next to the King's summer mansion in Clos, France.

This residence previously belonged to the king’s sister, Marguerite. The king was said to have visited the painter there and Leonardo was said to have appeared occasionally at the French court. Such a time corresponded to Anne Boleyn's time in Clos. Thus, it was likely that Anne Boleyn would have come into contact with the master artist during her time in France.

To support this conjecture, there exists a letter Anne wrote in 1514. She was at the time in Mechelen, Belgium which was a twin city of Antwerp. According to most historians, Anne was 13 (some claim only 7 years old). I agree that she was 13. In Antwerp and Mechelen there were artists who had received training by Leonardo in Milan. The key one was Joos van Cleve who is known as the Leonardo of the North. It would have been possible that someone of Anne's social stature would have met Joos van Cleve. His descriptions of Leonardo would have led her to hope to meet him one day. During the time Leonardo was residing at Clos Luce, Anne could easily have paid him a visit from the King's mansion, Château d'Amboise, where she likely spent her summers from 1516 through 1519 when Leonardo died.

Another possibility could have occurred in late 1515. As a maid of honor to Queen Claude of France, she may have traveled with the Queen for "pomp and circumstances". Anne was with the Queen until 1522 (age 21 or 15). Leonardo was part of Pope Leo X's peace delegation of 19Dec1515. If the Queen was there, then Anne was likely there as well. How interesting that would be if it happened that Anne and Leonardo had a conversation.

In my book about Leonardo, I suggest that Leonardo received an initiation from a hierophantic line emanating from George Gimestus Plethon. If so, then Leonardo likely would have seen something in this young woman's destiny. Some art historians have concluded that such a meeting did occur and that Leonardo's painting, *La Belle Ferronnière*, is a portrait of Anne Boleyn.

Martin Luther

The start of the Reformation is typically tied to Martin Luther's posting of his 95 theses on the door of All Saints Church in Wittenberg on October 31, 1517. The Theses were translated and distributed throughout Germany and Europe. Luther was a professor of moral theology at the University of Wittenberg,

Germany. As a professor, Luther had the privilege to invite interested scholars to participate in an academic inquiry. Instead, his ecclesiastical superiors tried and convicted him of heresy. For this, he was excommunication in 1521. Over the next 25 years, Luther expanded his points of needed Church reformation. During this time, many clergy and congregants joined the movement holding their own services. With monarch support, Lutheranism spread through all of Scandinavia during the sixteenth century. Through Baltic-German and Swedish rule, Lutheranism also spread into Estonia and Latvia. Since 1520, Lutheran services have been regularly held in Copenhagen.

On 6 March 1522, Luther secretly returned to Wittenberg. He wrote to the Elector: "During my absence, Satan has entered my sheepfold, and committed ravages which I cannot repair by writing, but only by my personal presence and living word."[212] For eight days in Lent, beginning on March 9, 1522, Luther preached sermon each day. These became known as the "Invocavit Sermons" because they began on

---

[212] Philip Schaff, *History of the Christian Church*, Vol VII, Ch IV; Letter of 7Mar1522, Brecht

Invocavit Sunday. His sermons warned the congregation not to turn to violence to bring about reforms. He spoke about love, patience, charity, and freedom as true Christian values.

Luther would later write that when he posted the 95 Theses, he was at that time a "papist". He did not expect that his Theses and its emphasis on indulgences would become a break with established Roman Catholic Church and its doctrine. The controversy propelled Luther to the leadership position of a movement that would later be called the Reformation.

Christian-on-Christian Wars of the Sixteenth Century

The Sacking of Rome

In 1527, there "was one of the most shocking and horrific assaults on Rome—and we know about it in great detail. For 10 months the city was occupied by the mutinous army of Emperor Charles V, killing, raping, kidnapping and torturing Romans. Thousands died. Matters were made worse because a large portion of the soldiers were Lutherans who felt a passionate hatred of Rome's Churchmen. The altar of St. Peter's was piled with corpses of those who had sought sanctuary there and for months the basilica was used as stables by the Imperial cavalry. Scores of clerics were branded, tortured or castrated. Today visitors can see the Castel Sant'Angelo, where Pope Clement VII escaped to, safe from the horror below. Of the assault itself, signs are few. In the Vatican Palace one can still see, scratched into plaster of a fresco by Raphael, the name Luther, written by one of Charles V's soldiers. And there is the Sistine Chapel. Michelangelo's ceiling paintings seem light and optimistic compared to disturbing, broody masterpiece, The Last Judgement. He painted the ceiling well before the sack but produced the Last Judgement after its terrors. One of the clearest signs of the 1527 sacking, though, is absence. Many European cities still have a few medieval timber houses but not Rome. Before the 1527 attack it had had thousands. Charles V's soldiers ripped out timbers, doors and frames to burn as firewood, speeding Rome's transformation to the city of fine stone homes."[213]

---

[213] Matthew Kneale, *Rome: A History in Seven Sackings*, Simon & Schuster, 2018

Peasants' War

The pent-up anger at the Church brought radicals into the movement. Men such as Müntzer in Thuringia plus Hipler and Lotzer in southwest Germany led the revolts that quickly turned into peasants' war. They believed that attacking the upper classes in general was necessary for a real Reformation. Revolts broke out in Franconia, Swabia, and Thuringia in 1524.

While Luther sympathized with their grievances, he strongly opposed their violence. During a tour of Thuringia, he became enraged at the widespread burning of convents, monasteries, bishops' palaces, and libraries. He thus wrote *Against the Murderous, Thieving Hordes of Peasants* upon his return to Wittenberg. In that article, he condemned the violence as the devil's work while giving his interpretation of wealth according to the Gospels.

Schmalkaldic War

Luther died in 1546. He would have condemned the Schmalkaldic War that began as a conflict between two German Lutheran rulers in 1547. It escalated to involve other Lutheran groups and the Catholic church.

The roots of this war go back to the 1521 Diet of Worms where Holy Roman Empire and Spanish Emperor Charles V had Martin Luther banned and the proliferation of his writings prohibited. The Diet condemned Luther and officially banned citizens of the Holy Roman Empire from defending or propagating his ideas. To encourage fulfillment of this decree, anyone who accused another of being an advocate of Lutheranism received half of the forfeited property with the other half going to the imperial government. No wonder citizens would call for a separation of Church and State.

The war broke out in Swabia when a group Lutheran rebels occupied the Catholic town of Füssen. Both Duke William IV of Bavaria and the Austrian Archduke Ferdinand I of Habsburg declared themselves neutral in the conflict. This allowed Charles V to strike with his Imperial army without condemnation.

In October of 1546, Duke Maurice of Saxony invaded the lands of his rival and cousin in Ernestine Saxony, both Lutherans. John Frederick I quickly came from Swabia and liberated Ernestine Saxony with his army. But he did not stop there, electing to invade the adjacent Lutheran Bohemian lands. The onset of winter left the armed conflict inconclusive.

When winter ended, Charles V set forth with his army for Bohemia on 28 March 1547. He united his forces with his brother's, King Ferdinand I of Bohemia. John Frederick I expected the Bohemian Lutherans to see this as a Lutheran-Catholic War and support him, but they did not. So, he was forced to retreat. Then on April 24, 1547, John Frederick I was taken prisoner at the Battle of Mühlberg.

After the battle of Mühlberg, the Lutheran cities Bremen and Magdeburg continued to resist the rule of Charles V. With 12,000 imperial soldiers, Duke Eric II of Brunswick-Calenberg unsuccessfully laid siege to Bremen from January until May. A Protestant army of the Schmalkaldic League approached. Duke Eric II and his Imperial forces went to confront the army. During the fighting, Eric was forced to swim over the Weser river in order to save himself. As a consequence of the Battle of Drakenburg of May 23, 1547, the Imperial troops left northern Germany.

But the conflict was not over. On May 15, 1548 Charles V decreed the Augsburg Interim that was to lead to the reintegration of the Protestants back into the Catholic Church. The edict provoked another revolt by the Protestant princes in 1552 and the Schmalkaldic War resumed. This time, with support from King Henry II of France, the Protestant army defeated Charles V who was forced to cancel his decrees and free John Frederick I of Saxony and Philip I of Hesse. Three years later the Peace of Augsburg was signed. The next year, Charles V voluntarily abdicated in favor of his brother Ferdinand I.

Thirty Year War

72 years after Luther's death, the Thirty-Year War began pitting, at first, Catholics against Protestants. Between 1618 and 1648, over 8 million people would die from the conflict. Most of the causalities were inflicted on the German population. It was one of the most destructive conflicts in human history. Initially this war was between the Protestant and Catholic states within the Holy Roman Empire, but it grew into a general European war. Gradually, it became less about religion and more about the French – Habsburg rivalry for European political dominance.

Tensions between Protestants and Catholics was already high when Ferdinand II was elected as the new Holy Roman Emperor. Ferdinand II was a strong supporter of the Catholic Church. When he tried to impose religious uniformity on his subjects, the Protestant states of northern Germany formed the Protestant Union to defend their interests. Bohemian Protestants then elected Frederick V, Elector Palatine, as the new king of the Kingdom of Bohemia. In response, the Catholic states of southern Germany formed the Catholic League. The Bohemian Revolt was crushed by the Catholic League at the Battle of White Mountain in 1620. The Protestant Union was dissolved in 1621. The last Protestant resistance was crushed at the Battle of Stadtlohn in 1623.

The defeat and treatment of the Protestants drew nearby Protestant countries into the war. Denmark intervened from 1625–1630 but was unsuccessful. Next the King of Sweden, Gustavus Adolphus, with the financial support of Catholic France entered the war. Although France was Catholic, they sought to undermine the Habsburg rulers of the Holy Roman Empire. The Swedes had driven deep into Catholic territory in southern Germany when

Gustavus Adolphus was killed at the Battle of Lützen in 1632. The advantage in the war swung back to the Catholics until France entered the war in 1635 – on the side of the Protestants! Now the religious struggle turned into a general European war.

Much of the death of The Thirty Years' War came from starvation and disease. Many regions were devastated. The armies, composed mainly of mercenaries, sought to fund themselves by looting the occupied territories because the war had bankrupted most of the combatant monarchies. Christian on Christian cruelty captioned each day. Exhausted morally and financially, the Peace of Westphalia in 1648 finally put an end to this devastating war.

Theology after the Renaissance

During the time and place of the Renaissance, Roman Catholicism was the only religion save a few Jewish communities. The primary philosophy was humanism that placed knowledge of the human being as central all knowledge. Renaissance humanism revived aspects of Hellenism in its study of Greek philosophers and classical antiquity. It embraced the concept that each human was a microcosm of the macrocosm. In their pursuit of knowledge, Humanists, in their love of learning, bought books and built libraries. It sought to educate the citizenry to be able to speak and write with eloquence and clarity and thereby be capable of engaging in the civic life building communities. An outcome was that grammar, rhetoric, history, poetry, and moral philosophy became the ingredients for a study in the humanities.

Following the Renaissance came the Reformation. The average citizen had achieved some basic education that hitherto was reserved for monks. Bible translations became available. Egoism as the twin of individual intellect, saw diminishing value in being led by an institution that had fallen deep into corruption. Religious unity was the casualty of "I know".

Then theology, in the West, became greatly simplified. The struggles over the Trinity, their substance(s), the Filioque, and the composition or members of the human being were settled. Materialism had crept into all aspects of theology. One can readily see this in the depiction of angels and archangels in art. In Baroque art, cute, winged infants were used to romanticize a scene. The wingless angels of Renaissance art had fallen under the weight of materialism. Soon thereafter, all spiritual beings, save Christ, disappear altogether from both art and theology. Christ, who had become the only God, then became, towards the end of the nineteenth century, just an interesting man. Lastly, in the twentieth century, Science, now separated from art and religion, managed to reduce its own as well as general philosophy to 'we don't need God anymore.'

Science and Religion (and Art) had split apart. Science claimed the territory of the Lifeless while Religion claimed that of the soul. Art was left homeless and began to wander seeking realism in landscapes to Impressionism, to Expressionism, to Cubism, and Modern Art. Science would later claim Reality and its ability to explain it without any concepts of God. It enjoyed its freedom from Religion.

The push to educate one's citizenry, led to battles on what to teach. Into the middle of the nineteenth century, the Bible was considered a major component of one's Western education. In America, this became a major issue when the population expanded from its Protestant base (e.g., Puritans) to include Catholics. Schools were funded through taxes. Catholic children were not allowed to be taught the Bible. Instead, there was a prepared catechism for their religious education. Getting nowhere to install this in the existing schools, Catholics set up their own schools and then requested appropriate tax revenues. Rather than negotiating, in some cases the homes of Catholics were burned such as the Philadelphia Nativist riots of 1844.[214] [215] The school movement of this period was called the Common School movement inspired by Horace Mann. In 1839, Mann oversaw the establishment in Lexington, Massachusetts of the first teacher training institute whose goal was to produce standardized, methodological teaching practices. Fundamental to this teaching was the development of morality. In response to the objections of Catholics, the Common School modified its teaching to be able to claim it was inspired by but not intended to be overtly Biblical in its words or practices. The Common School curriculum evolved to stress

---

[214] Elizabeth M. Geffen, "Violence in Pennsylvania in the 1840s and 1850s." Pennsylvania History 36.4, 1969
[215] Patrick Grubbs, "Riots (1830s and 1840s)" *Encyclopedia of Greater Philadelphia*, 2018

the "Three R's" (***r***eading, w***r***iting, and a***r***ithmetic) plus history, geography, and math. In the coming century, Religion faded while the non-controversial science of the Lifeless took its place.

Heretics During and After the Renaissance

Well after Leonardo's death, heretics continued to die for their beliefs. But now the scope of heresy hunting widened from theologists and Christian sects to scientists, especially astronomers who dealt with the "heavens".

The Astronomers and Their Heresies

Papal decrees against astronomers Copernicus, Galileo, Kepler, and others would not be lifted until 1835. Until then, Catholics were forbidden to study anything relating to the Copernican or heliocentric view. The geocentric model put the human-spirit as primary in the model and the orbits. For determination of the orbits of the physical planets, the heliocentric model was well known to Greek, Egyptian, and Babylonian astronomers. But of interest to these ancients was what today we call astrology and the influence of the celestial forces upon the human and life on Earth. Thus, the geocentric model fit their needs best. As this feeling for celestial influences diminished under the weight of materialism, the need to make the heliocentric model primary arose. Let's look at some of these astronomers, their lives, their intentions, and the punishments for their so-called heresies. We will see the erosion of Religion's territory to Science and how Religion resisted this shift.

Giordano Bruno (1548 – 1600) At 17, he entered the Dominican order in Naples. Upon being admitted, he changed his name from Filippo Bruno after Giordano Crispo who was his tutor in metaphysics. Since this was where Thomas Aquinas had once taught, his monastic studies naturally led into Scholasticism and Aristotelianism. True to the Renaissance Age, Bruno was attracted to the ancient philosophies including Plato and Hermes Trismegistus. He was regarded as a brilliant, free thinker but his interest in forbidden books caused him monastic difficulties. But when his interest in the heretical Arian theology and the banned writings of Erasmus were discovered, he fled the monastery, shedding his religious habit. He wandered for nearly seven years until he settled for a time in Toulouse, France (a former Cathar city). There he completed his doctorate in theology. His talents got him elected by the students to lecture in philosophy. When religious strife broke out in the summer of 1581, he moved to Paris. There he held a cycle of thirty lectures on theological topics, but it was his fame for his prodigious memory that saved his career. These talents came to the attention of King Henry III who summoned him for a demonstration. Of this, Bruno wrote, "I got me such a name that King Henry III summoned me one day to discover from me if the memory which I possessed was natural or acquired by magic art. I satisfied him that it did not come from sorcery but from organized *knowledge*; and, following this, I got a book on memory printed, entitled *The Shadows of Ideas*, which I dedicated to His Majesty. Forthwith he gave me an Extraordinary Lectureship with a salary."[216]

While in Paris, powerful French patrons protected Bruno. During this period, he published several works. Most of these were about his mnemonic method of organized knowledge and experience. The

---

[216] William Boulting, *Giordano Bruno: His Life, Thought, and Martyrdom*, p. 58, 1916 (Amazon Services 2015)

recommendation from Henry III sent him to England in 1583 to be the guest of the French ambassador, Michel de Castelnau. There he became involved with members of John Dee's circle known for their alchemy and Hermetic practices. He was given a temporary post to lecture at Oxford. Here he had several works published, including those on Cosmology and his views on an infinite universe. His views on philosophy, science, and religion were controversial for those times. One opponent was George Abbot, who later became Archbishop of Canterbury. Abbot ridiculed his heliocentric view, "the opinion of Copernicus that the earth did go round, and the heavens did stand still; whereas in truth it was his own head which rather did run round, and his brains did not stand still".[217] Abbot went further to claim that Bruno had misrepresented Ficino's work, even plagiarize it. This attack as well as his loss of friends who grew uncomfortable with his controversies drove Bruno to return to the continent.

He eventually was invited to come to Padua. Here he taught briefly as he sought,

---

[217] Andrew D. Weiner, "Expelling the Beast: Bruno's Adventures in England", Modern Philology, 78, Aug. 1980

unsuccessfully, for the chair of mathematics (which went to Galileo Galilei). Struggling, Bruno accepted an invitation to tutor Señor Zuane Mocenigo in Venice. In 1592 he arrived and taught for two months. Neither Bruno nor his host were happy with this arrangement. When Bruno announced his plan to leave this post, his host denounced him to the Venetian Inquisition. Bruno was arrested in May 1592. The Roman Inquisition then asked for him to be transferred to be tried in Rome. Bruno was sent to Rome in February 1593. His trial lasted seven years. During this time, he was held in jail, notably the Tower of Nona. Charges included blasphemy, immoral conduct, but the most damning were heresy in matters of dogmatic theology. On January 20, 1600, Bruno was declared a heretic by Pope Clement VIII. The Inquisition then issued a sentence of death. On Ash Wednesday, February 17, 1600, in the central Roman market square, Bruno was stripped of his clothes, hung upside down, and burned at the stake.

Always trying to stay one step ahead of the Inquisition, he moved frequently. When lured to an academic position in Padua, Italy, he was arrested and sent to Rome where he endured a seven-year trial whose outcome was to burn him alive. What was his crime? He proposed a heliocentric solar system.

Philosophers admired Bruno, but picked through his works selecting some and rejecting those tending towards the occult or to Hermetic magic. Of his six written dialogues: three are cosmological and three moral. His saw the solar system as heliocentric as opposed to the geocentric view held by the Church. His theory also led to an infinite universe composed of innumerable stars with planets similar to our solar system. His monistic theory places form and matter as polarities of a oneness. Spirit would set form. He opposed the dualism of the Aristotelian physics that was embedded in Church philosophy and dogma.

John Dee (1527 – 1609) was the Renaissance Man of England. He was considered to be the wisest man of his day in many fields including mathematics, astronomy, astrology, as well as various occult fields alchemy, magic, Hermetic philosophy. Dee collected a large variety of books amassing one of England's largest libraries. Because of his interest in the occult fields, he was viewed with suspicion by some and admiration by others, especially Queen Elizabeth I.

His scholarly status had pulled him into Elizabethan politics as an adviser to many ministers. He tutored and patronized Sir Philip Sidney to whom Bruno dedicated one of his works. During much of his last 30 years, he sought to commune with angels intending to learn the universal language of those involved in the creation. He expected through this to understand the purpose of human evolution as well as the creative source of the Logos that he felt was the archetype of mankind. He drew heavily from Marsilio Ficino and the other teachers of the Platonic Academy of Florence. For Dee, there should be no distinction between natural science and spiritual science. He expected to discover a spiritual structure from divine forms to the sense perceptible world that is both transcendent and emergent.

Galileo Galilei (1564 – 1642) argued for a heliocentric model of the solar system when most subscribed to either a geo-centric model or to that of Tycho Brahe. Galileo's Copernicanism was met with opposition from astronomers and from the Church. His writings were investigated by the Roman Inquisition in

1615. They concluded that heliocentrism was "foolish and absurd in philosophy, and formally heretical since it explicitly contradicts in many places the sense of Holy Scripture."[218]

Galileo was defended by the Jesuits and Pope Urban VIII until he wrote *Dialogue Concerning the Two Chief World Systems* in 1632. While not explicit, he lost this support when he appeared to attack the Pope. He was subsequently tried by the Inquisition and found to be "vehemently suspect of heresy." He was essentially forced to recant or lose his life. The court placed him under house arrest where he spent the rest of his life. During these later years at home, he wrote *Two New Sciences* in which he summarized his work in kinematics and material science.

"One should recall that the Church gained opprobrium in the eyes of posterity for marginalising Galileo's book on the two world systems, on the grounds that Copernicanism, which promoted the idea of a moving earth, was inconvenient to teach to credulous masses of people. Science could not be permitted to say in the seventeenth century that the ground

---

[218] James Hannam, *The Genesis of Science*, Regnery, 2011, pp. 329–344.

beneath people's feet was rushing along because if that were so, how could anything, even the Church, be secure? Thus, it was not purely scientific considerations that led to Galileo's silencing. Rather, it was political ones and it seems it is also not scientific reasons that cause a modern man to renounce the possibility that he and his earth body are the centre of the universe or that human beings are, after all the central subject of all science."[219]

Johannes Kepler (1571 – 1630) was a contemporary of Galileo. Known for his Laws of Planetary Motion, Kepler remained a very religious man believing that God had created our world according to an intelligible plan. He was a believer in the path of knowledge claiming one can come to understand God's plan. For him and most others in the profession of this time, there was no clear distinction between astronomy and astrology. The stars were homes to spiritual beings that affected our lives. Kepler described his new astronomy as "celestial physics." Of his own reasoning, he called it "an excursion into

---

[219] Sandra Moore, Science and Mathematics Group of the Anthroposophical Society in Great Britain, Newsletter, March 2018

Aristotle's Metaphysics" and his conclusions "a supplement to Aristotle's *On the Heavens*."

Invisible College (~1640 – 1660) began as a circle of scholars who secretly met face-to-face according to the norms of Rosicrucianism. They studied Greek philosophers, exchanged ideas, and collaborated with each other. But word of the college spread. As it spread, the members realized they needed to become a public scientific institution. It was destined to become the Royal Society of London. Robert Boyle was instrumental for this transition.

Nothing certain is known of the origin, however, letters by Boyle in 1646 and 1647 refer to "our invisible college". Robert Boyle was an alchemist but is known today as the father of modern chemistry. Other prominent scientists involved included Sir Cheney Culpeper, Isaac Marcombes, Francis Tallents, Samuel Hartliband, John Dury, and Benjamin Worsley who had become the "prime mover" of the Invisible College in the 1640s. By November 1660, the transition was complete as the Royal Society was granted then a royal charter by King Charles II.

12. Conclusion

This book has been built upon the premise that Marsilio Ficino and members of the Platonic Academy of Florence, including artists such as Leonardo da Vinci, became aware in their thirst for knowledge of its ancient flow from the Mysteries into Hellenism and hence on into the various Christian theologies. Since the time of Augustine (354-430), Faith had wrested control of Christianity away from Knowledge. Gnosticism was overthrown. This passion for knowledge was ignited by Gemistus Plethon's lectures on metaphysics and on the Greek mysteries while he as in Florence. This passion gave birth to the Florentine awakening that cultivated the Renaissance. This became a real blossoming of Knowledge during the Renaissance. With renewed strength, it engaged in battle again with Faith for control of Christianity. Intellectuality had become a capacity for every person. But unseen, materialism had permeated Knowledge. Yet the burgeoning intellect offered a sense of freedom, freedom to think beyond the boundaries of religion, art, and science. Such intellectual freedom, the realization that "I think" rather than "it thinks in me", gave momentum to the Reformation. It continues into modern times with the feeling that one needs church only for community and no longer for one's spiritual interests or pursuits.

The theology adhered to by the fifteenth century Roman Catholic Church had evolved greatly since its roots in proto-Orthodoxy. Ecumenical Councils had established Church dogma. Fourth to seventh century heresy hunting had driven most scholars of the ancient wisdom towards the more accepting East. Charlemagne's envoys had returned from their journey to Harun al Rachid with teachers from the great schools around Baghdad. These were joined by unusual scholars for England and Ireland when Charlemagne set all of these to work to establish a system of education. Hence, he became known as the Father of French education. Their work streamed into the School of Chartres where Alanus ab Insulis (Alain de Lille, 1128 – 1203), John of Salisbury (1120 – 1180), and others gave new life within Christianity to Plato and the other Greek philosophers. Mysticism too was rebirthed. Then Scholasticism, under Thomas Aquinas and his teacher Albertus Magnus (1200 – 1280) had the fertile soil upon which it could sow the seeds for the Renaissance. To his contemporaries, Aquinas' teacher, Albert the

Great, was a wizard of magic. It was said that he was a "teacher of everything there is to know."

Throughout this book, the esoteric foundations to various streams of Christianity were repeatedly rising up only to be dealt with by brutal means. Before the time of Christ, the ancient Mysteries had faded away. They had slipped into decadence as individual intelligence arose and along with it, egoism. In the change from the fourth to the fifth century, Augustine, who had studied the ancient Mysteries along with their scholars and the Greek philosophers, called these predecessors as Christian before the term Christianity had come into being. Early Christianity, according to *Secret Mark*, continued the practice of secrecy with its new form of initiation. The raising of Lazarus was an ancient initiation done in public with Christ as the hierophant. Thus, Lazarus, a new man, takes on the name John (the Evangelist). The initiation of Saul, who subsequently changed his name to Paul, was the first of the new Christian initiations.

History has shown multiple generations of esoteric Christian groups freely offering their gifts only to become martyrs. Following the threat to Roman Catholicism by the Cathars, a Holy Inquisition was established to root out all remnants following a crusade intended to wipe out all Cathar communities. Yet esoteric Christianity lived on. Johann Gottlieb Fichte, in 1806 wrote, "Despite for the most part being misunderstood and persecuted by the established church, we assert that this knowledge, in all its integrity and purity, and which we are incapable of surpassing, has in every age and since the origin of Christianity still been able to prevail and flourish in secret here and there [...] though this doctrine may appear new and unprecedented in the present epoch, it is actually as old as the world, and it is especially the doctrine of Christianity that can be found in the most genuine and purest ancient document, in the Gospel of John, which up until this moment is present before our eyes; and this doctrine is even expounded there using exactly the same images and expressions that we employ."[220] The Cathars would have agreed to this claim. It is why each member carried the Gospel of John, the

[220] Johann Gottlieb Fichte, *The Way to the Blessed Life* (1806), trans. W. Smith (London: John Chapman, 1849)

initiated Lazarus, with them wherever they went.

Esoteric Secrets Hidden in Plain Sight

In 1913, Rudolf Steiner, in speaking to an audience about esoteric knowledge, said "What I am about to say is extreme heresy from the point of view of our time. For example, there is nothing better protected in the regions of Central Europe than Fichte's philosophy. Not that it is kept secret, for his teachings are printed and are read. But they are not understood. They remain secrets. In this way much that will have to enter the general development of mankind will remain occult knowledge though it is published and revealed in the light of day."[221] Our concepts established during our education leave us blind to esotericism. What was once considered a betrayal of the Mysteries, is now put into art, movies, print, and online media for anyone, but our blindness prevents it from being seen consciously unless an inner awakening has previously occurred.

---

[221] Rudolf Steiner, *The Occult Significance of the Bhagavad Gita*, lecture 8, 4Jun1913, GA 146

Renaissance 2.0

With the words "To develop a complete mind: study the science of art; study the art of science. Learn how to see. Realize that everything connects to everything else"[222] Leonardo da Vinci set the goal for the first Renaissance. He went back to earlier ages of history for answers. Humanism of the Renaissance arose in the evolution of the spiritual life. Humanism became the object of men's striving, not because they had grasped the human in his or her essential nature, but because they had lost the spiritual reality of the human.

Nature became the field of the revelations of the senses. But it has been studied materialistically. The forms of Nature no longer were perceived as the work of the Divine. Nature became something devoid of spirit. But the human thinks. What was thinking? Once felt to be a spiritual activity, this too fell to materialism. Direct vision of the Spirit working in the past was discredited. Any vision of the Spirit in the present was denied as possible or suitable for Scientific inquiry.

---

[222] https://www.goodreads.com/quotes/1423493-to-develop-a-complete-mind-study-the-science-of-art

Since the Renaissance, the best minds in the West have evolved ideas in the scientific and social fields. These ideas have been applied to history, science, philosophy, technology, even to the mystical. All of these represented the striving to find, in what has now become an intellectualistic world-conception, the true nature of the human being. But, until now, all such ideas were dimmed, were colored by the boundaries natural science gave itself, namely the Lifeless. In order to study something, it is reduced to the Lifeless to be examined. Its emergent properties are thereby lost. Intellectuality was tied to only what the physical senses provided. The views of reality allowed nothing that the physical senses did not tell them.

Today we live in a time that calls for a new renaissance not only of knowledge but also of morality that in the end Art, Science, and Religion can overlap one another once again. As Gus Speth put it when discussing how to prevent climate change, "I used to think the top environmental problems were biodiversity loss, ecosystem collapse, and climate change. I thought that with 30 years of good science, we could address those problems. But I was wrong. The top environmental problems are selfishness, greed, and apathy. And to deal with those we need a spiritual and cultural transformation – and we scientists don't know how to do that."[223]

To commence such a major change, we must begin with our model of the human being. This model has lost its spirit, and, for most academics, its soul too is no longer understood. By the mid-twentieth century, following WW II, human consciousness was viewed as nothing more than a bio-chemical reaction to sensory stimuli. Free will was considered by academics as an illusion. Everything could be explained as the result of particles by science. Emotions were merely the effect from hormones. Such a philosophy for science and humanity, makes life meaningless. It naturally leads to a new Epicureanism where one aspires to a workless life while being continuously entertained by a flow of images on a screen and pre-prepared food.

Will our era have its own Leonardo to initiate a new Renaissance? Will there be a renewal of

---

[223] James Gustave Speth, 2007 Yale Forum on Religion and Ecology, quoted by Rev. Ken Wilson to the Miami Herald 18Feb2010, see http://fore.yale.edu/files/2010_UNEP_emails.pdf

the arts, of the sciences, and religion too? Will they be able to act together for the progress of the cultural life? Will knowledge of the human being as body, soul, and spirit arise again?

"Just as mankind has to do with the three realms of nature, he also has to do with three spiritual realms. Now you may say: It is of no consequence whether I believe it or not, for these three kingdoms are not visible, not perceptible. Yes, my friends, I have known people [circa 1880s] to whom it had to be explained that air exists! They could not believe that there was something like air. When I say to such a person, this is a table – that he can believe, for when he goes to the table, he can knock on the table, and when he looks at it, he sees the table with his own eyes, but he cannot bump into the air. He looks around and says, there is nothing here. However, everyone nowadays admits the existence of air. The existence of air is simply accepted.

"In the same way, it will happen that people will come to admit the existence of a spiritual world. Today, people still say: The spiritual realm simply does not exist – in the same manner that the peasants used to say: There is no air. In my native village, the peasants used

to say: there is no air at all, only the big-headed people from the city assert that because they want to give the impression that they are so clever; one can walk through it because there is nothing to walk through! – But that was long ago. Today [1924], farmers also accept that air exists. But even the smartest people still don't recognize that there are spiritual beings everywhere! They will, however, acknowledge it in due time, because otherwise certain things simply will be inexplicable, things that will need to be understood."[224]

Nowadays heretics are not dealt with by burnings or poisonings. A modern-day sentence of being exiled from scientific publications or academic community still exists. Yet, change is happening. The property of emergence is gaining strength in biology and physics. Pioneers once looked at as fools and dreamers whose words are only the product of a capricious imagination, are finding acceptance. Once ridiculed by the high court of scientific judgement, they are finding ways to build upon existing science and harmonize

---

[224] Rudolf Steiner, *Die Geschichte der Menschheit und die Weltanschauungen der Kulturvölker,* Dornach, 25Jun1924, GA 353, pg. 306

with what might be called spiritual science or a science of the Living.

I expect that a spiritual science, when developed, can illuminate Life by showing that there is an immortal core to each human being. That when one passes through death into the spiritual worlds, this individual enters a different consciousness as it sojourns from death until it returns to physical existence to gather new experiences not only for its own evolution but for that of other spiritual beings as well. These fruits of life are carried up through death into spiritual worlds.

"We would see how the bonds established from one person to another, from soul to soul in all areas of life, those attractions of the heart that pass from soul to soul and from which there is otherwise no explanation, can be explained by the fact that they were formed through relationships in former lives. We would also see that the inner spiritual bonds we form today also do not come to an end when death moves over the face of our earthly existence. Instead, what moves from soul to soul as a bond of life is as immortal as the human soul itself. It continues to live with the soul as the latter passes through the spiritual world, and it

will come to life again in other future earthly relationships and new incarnations. It is only a question of evolution until people will remember their earlier earthly experiences and what they lived through in former earth lives and conditions of existence."[225]

A new Renaissance requires a new Humanism that sees the Human again as microcosm of the macrocosm. A new science must feel comfortable overlapping with religion and with art. Knowledge derived from the Hellenist (and earlier) model of the human being as body, soul, and spirit would become a spiritual science. To perform such research, the scientist will need to develop slumbering human capacities in order to experience the Living. This will ignite a new passion for knowledge of the human being. We can no longer find satisfaction for this quest in what the present is able to provide.

Final Thoughts

Through a few Renaissance individuals, such as Gemistus Plethon, Marsilio Ficino, and Leonardo da Vinci, and others, Knowledge was

---

[225] Rudolf Steiner, *Goethe's Faust*, 23Jan1910, GA 272, pg. 19-20

returned to its throne. Faith was overthrown. Leonardo da Vinci proclaimed "For, verily, great love springs from great knowledge of the beloved object, and if you little know it, you will be able to love it only little or not at all."[226] Leonardo was a lover of Sophia, i.e. Wisdom. Science must rediscover the Wisdom that forms the Human.

Leonardo added, "Learning acquired in youth arrests the evil of old age; and if you understand that old age has wisdom for its food, you will so conduct yourself in youth that your old age will not lack for nourishment."[227]

Leonardo earned the title The Renaissance Man through his love of wisdom that united Art, Science, and Religion. Today we await the next Leonardo to take us into Renaissance 2.0. In Leonardo's time, wisdom was crippled by Church dogma. Today, wisdom is once again crippled, this time by the Church of Materialism. But the various scientific fields have reached the boundary of materialism. The next Leonardo will become a bridge to carry Art, Science, and Religion beyond the

---

[226] https://www.leonardodavinci.net/quotes.jsp

[227] https://www.leonardodavinci.net/quotes.jsp

boundaries of materialism to the next spiritual and cultural transformation.

Although St. Paul described the human as a being of body, soul, and spirit,[228] over the centuries the human constitution was reduced by dogma to body and soul. The eternal quality of spirit was deemed to be only attainable as a reward by the righteous on Judgment Day. In our time, it has become a form of scientific heresy for an educated person to speak about spirit or soul as realities. The concept "human" has been reduced today to body alone. With such a starved concept, no wonder today's Transhumanists can entertain images of future that no longer needs the human.

The Science hopefully will now expand beyond its limits within the Lifeless to include the Living. This will spur a new Renaissance based on new knowledge of the human as microcosm of the macrocosm. Then Science and Religion will find common ground to mutually benefit each other when the scientist reveres his or her lab bench like an altar and where he or she

---

[228] 1 Thessalonians 5:23, Paul refers to human nature as consisting of soma, psyche, and pneuma; that is body, soul, and spirit respectively.

can see their experimental phenomena with the eyes of an artist.[229]

[229] This is a paraphrase from a similar statement by Rudolf Steiner, The Human Soul in Relation to Sun and Moon, 7May1922, GA 212

Epilogue

This book has illustrated repeated sins and high crimes against those Christians who had a different theology than the established one. Might made right. If it is possible to put aside the moral outrage of these sins and high crimes, then it is possible to see meaning in the theological battles of the past 2000 years.

Indeed, this is possible. This book has shown that humanity as a whole once lived within ethnic groupings that had a collective consciousness that was led by the initiates of their mystery center. As individual intelligence arose, these mystery centers faded. At the time of the Christ event, these mystery centers had become decadent when compared to their glory years. The early years of Christianity still saw some initiations as described in *Secret Mark*. The author of *Revelations* clearly claimed to be such an initiate who could directly experience the spiritual world. But this too faded.

Multiple streams of Christianity existed in the first couple centuries following the event on Golgotha. The path of knowledge itself became decadent and fraught with pride and egoism. Against this came Augustine who attempted to find a path to God for the common man. Faith became the hallmark of Augustine's new Christian path.

Until the 13th century, initiates still incarnated who could achieve some insights but by the middle of the 13th century, no human was capable any more of reaching the spiritual world. It has closed so that humanity could develop freedom, freedom to perform moral deeds out of love. This closing of the doors to heaven lasted until about 1900. Materialism grew and flourished in this period.

Are we now experiencing a rebirth of these first century Christianities? Perhaps, but I sense the larger picture is that we are in a time where the individualism is moving from "I think" to "I feel" and to "I will". For each human, this age blots out Nature as a source for spiritual awakening or insights. Our Technological Age physically isolates humans from other humans and from Nature. Many are finding community not with those nearby but with those that they interact with online. Although the spatial boundary is fading, isolation from human warmth of soul is increasing.

Out of this isolation and the experience of a lifeless world, the spirit within our microcosm begins to speak. Our soul hears this speaking like the souls of old heard the gods within the mystery centers. We will gradually become conscious of our own constitution as comprised of body, soul, and spirit. With this, a new Christianity will emerge.

List of Figures

Bibliography

- Harold W. Attridge, *Eusebius, Early Christianity and Judaism*, Wayne State University Press, First Edition edition, 1992
- Carmen Bambach, *Leonardo da Vinci Rediscovered*, Yale University Press, 2019
- Nicola Barbatelli, Carlo Pedretti, *Leonardo a Donnaregina. I Salvator Mundi per Napoli*, Elio De Rosa Editore; CB Edizioni, 2017
- Richard Bauckham (Editor), Old Testament Pseudepigrapha: More Noncanonical Scriptures, Eerdmans, 2013
- Rachel Billinge, Luke Syson, and Marika Spring, 'Altered Angels: Two Panels from the Immaculate Conception Altarpiece once in San Francesco Grande, Milan'. National Gallery Technical Bulletin Vol 32, pp 57–77. http://www.nationalgallery.org.uk/technical-bulletin/billinge_syson_spring2011
- E. A. Wallis Budge, *Osiris and the Egyptian Resurrection*, P. L. Warner Books, 1911
- Tony Burke, *New Testament Apocrypha: More Noncanonical Scriptures*, Eerdmans, 2016

- James H. Charlesworth, *The Old Testament Pseudepigrapha* (2 Volume set), Hendrickson Publishers, 2010
- Angela Ottino della Chiesa, *The Complete Paintings of Leonardo da Vinci*, Penguin Classics, 1967
- Kenneth Clark and Martin Kemp, *Leonardo da Vinci*, The Folio Society, 2005
- April DeConick, *The Gnostic New Age: How a Countercultural Spirituality Revolutionized Religion from Antiquity to Today*, Columbia University Press, 2016
- Nicola Denzey Lewis, *Introduction to Gnosticism: Ancient Voices, Christian Worlds*, Oxford University Press, 2012
- Nicola Denzey Lewis, *Cosmology and Fate in Gnosticism and Graeco-Roman Antiquity: Under Pitiless Skies*, Brill, 2013
- Bart Ehrman, *The New Testament: A Historical Introduction to the Early Christian Writings*. Oxford University Press, 2015
- Bart Ehrman, *Jesus Before the Gospels. How the Earliest Christians Remembered, Changed, and Invented Stories of the Savior*, HarperOne, 2016
- Bart Ehrman, *The Orthodox Corruption of Scripture: The Effect of Early Christological*

Controversies on the Text of the New Testament, Oxford University Press, 1996

- J. K. Elliott, *The Apocryphal New Testament: A Collection of Apocryphal Christian Literature*, Oxford University Press, 2005
- Paula Fredriksen, *From Jesus to Christ: The Origins of the New Testament Images of Jesus*, Yale University Press; 2nd edition, 2008
- Tom Harpur, *The Pagan Christ*, Thomas Allen Publishers, 2004
- M. R. James (Editor), *The New Testament Apocrypha*, Apocryphile Press, 2004
- Rodolphe Kasser et al, *The Gospel of Judas*, Second Edition, National Geographic, 2008
- Martin Kemp, *Leonardo*, Oxford University Press, 2004
- Martin Kemp, *Leonardo da Vinci. The Marvellous Works of Nature and Man*, Oxford University Press, 2006
- Martin Kemp, *Leonardo by Leonardo*, Callaway A&E, 2019
- Helmut Koester, *Introduction to the New Testament, Vol. 2: History and Literature of Early Christianity*, de Gruyter, 2nd edition, 2000

- Marvin W. Meyer (Editor), *The Nag Hammadi Scriptures*, HarperOne, 2009
- Charles Nicholl, *Leonardo da Vinci: The Flights of the Mind*, Penguin, 2005
- Elaine Pagels, *The Gnostic Gospels*, Random House, 1979
- Carlo Pedretti, *Leonardo and the European Genius*, CB Edizioni, 2008
- Carlo Pedretti, *Leonardo Genius and Vision in the Land of Marches*, CB Edizioni, 2005
- Carlo Pedretti, *Leonardo da Vinci*, Taj Books, 2005
- E. Randolph Richards, *Paul and First-Century Letter-Writing: Secretaries, Composition and Collection*. Intervarsity Press, 2004
- Wilhelm Schneemelcher, *New Testament Apocrypha, Vol. 1: Gospels and Related Writings Revised Edition*, Westminster John Knox Press, 1990
- Wilhelm Schneemelcher, *New Testament Apocrypha, Vol. 2: Writings Relating to the Apostles Apocalypses and Related Subjects*, Westminster John Knox Press, 1992
- Rudolf Steiner, *Christianity as Mystical Fact*, Anthroposophic Press, 1972 (from 1910)

- Rudolf Steiner, *From Jesus to Christ*, Rudolf Steiner Press, 1973 (lectures from 1911)
- William Whiston (Editor), *The Works of Josephus*, Thomas Nelson, 2003
- Michael Williams, *Rethinking "Gnosticism": An Argument for Dismantling a Dubious Category*, Princeton University Press, 1996
- James VanderKam and Peter Flint, *The Meaning of the Dead Sea Scrolls*, HarperCollins, 2013
- Geza Vermes, *The Complete Dead Sea Scrolls in English*, Penguin Classics, 2012
- Giorgio Vasari (1568), *Lives of the Artists*. Penguin Classics, trans. George Bull 1965
- Frank Zöllner, *Leonardo da Vinci. The Complete Paintings*, Taschen, 2018
- Center for the Study of New Testament Manuscripts, http://csntm.org/About
- Early Christian Writings, http://www.earlychristianwritings.com/
- Open Culture, Leonardo's Notebook Pages Online: http://www.openculture.com/2017/07/leonardo-da-vincis-visionary-notebooks-now-online-browse-570-digitized-pages.html

Index

www.ingramcontent.com/pod-product-compliance
Lightning Source LLC
LaVergne TN
LVHW020525100826
845148LV00010B/1338

* 9 7 8 1 7 3 6 3 1 6 5 9 7 *